The Children's Encyclopedia *of* BIBLE BELIEFS

Written by Mark Water
Illustrations by Karen Donnelly

ZondervanPublishingHouse
Grand Rapids, Michigan

A Division of HarperCollinsPublishers

THE CHILDREN'S ENCYCLOPEDIA
OF BIBLE BELIEFS

COPYRIGHT © 1995 HUNT & THORPE
TEXT © MARK WATER
ILLUSTRATIONS © KAREN DONNELLY

Originally published by Hunt & Thorpe 1995

Designed by
THE BRIDGEWATER BOOK COMPANY
Designer *Sarah Bentley*
Managing Editor *Anna Clarkson*
Editor *Fiona Corbridge*
Page make-up *Chris Lanaway*
Text consultant *Derek Williams*

ISBN 0-310-21104-2

In the United States this book is published by:
Zondervan Publishing House
Grand Rapids, Michigan 49530

All rights reserved. Except for brief quotations in critical articles or reviews, no part of this book may be reproduced in any manner without prior permission from the publishers

Printed and bound in the USA

ACKNOWLEDGEMENTS
Bible quotations are from:
The Holy Bible, New International Version,
© 1973, 1978, 1984 by International Bible Society. Used by permission of Hodder and Stoughton. International Children's Bible, New Century Version (Anglicized Edition),
© 1991 Word (UK) Ltd. Used by permission.

CONTENTS

Angels: God's messengers	5
Anger: good and bad	6
Animals: caring for	7
Baptism: entering the Christian faith	8
Christian life: starting	9

Christian life: living	10
Christian life: witnessing	11
Church: a family	12
Church: one and many	13
Creation and evolution	14
Creed: what a Christian believes	15
Death and killing	16
Devil: the enemy of Christianity	17
Drugs and addictions	18
End of the world	19
Faith: a strong belief	20
Fame and ambition	21
Families today	22
Forgiveness from God	23
Forgiveness: forgiving one another	24
Freedom through Jesus	25
Friendship: caring and sharing	26
Ghosts and demons	27
Giving and taking	28
God: who is he?	29
God and his actions	30
God: looking for	31
Gossip and finding fault	32
Grace: God's love	33
Green issues	34
Guidance by dreams and signs	35

Guidance: making decisions	36
Happiness through Christian faith	37
Healing and health	38
Heaven and hell	39
Holiness	40
Holy Spirit: who is he?	41
Holy Spirit in the Bible	42
Holy Spirit at work today	43
Hope and endurance	44
Jesus: why he came	45
Jesus: the man	46
Jesus is alive	47

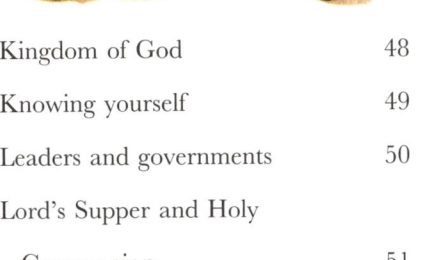

Kingdom of God	48
Knowing yourself	49
Leaders and governments	50
Lord's Supper and Holy Communion	51
Love	52
Marriage and divorce	53
Miracles: impossible things happen	54
Money: a root of evil?	55

Names, blasphemy, swearing	56
Obedience: obeying God	57
Peace	58
People in need: helping others	59
Persecution and bullying	60
Prayer: the Lord's	61
Prayer questions	62
Prayer problems	63
Prejudice: fighting against	64
Priests and prophets	65
Promises and agreements	66
Religions: other beliefs	67
Suffering	68
Sunday: a day of rest	69
Superstition and magic	70
Temptation	71
Ten Commandments: God's laws	72
Thanks and praise	73
Trinity of God	74
Truth and lies	75
Wisdom: 'wise as serpents'	76
Women	77
Work	78
Worship today	79
Index	80

ABOUT THIS BOOK

This book is like a dictionary. All the subjects are in alphabetical order. This means that you don't have to start at the beginning: you can start anywhere, depending on what you want to read about. The title at the top of each page gives you the main subject for that page. You can find which page you need by looking in the contents page, or in the index at the end of this book.

Many people argue about what Bible teaching means. What does the Bible say about Jesus Christ? Look up the headings, or look in the index to find out.

Enjoy the colourful, clearly drawn artwork – it shows you what people wore in Bible times, how they lived and travelled, and also what we think the different characters might have looked like.

Bible Search

- Abraham: *Romans 4:18–25*
- God's promise: *John 3:16–19*
- Heroes and heroines of faith: *Hebrews 11*
- A sick woman: *Mark 5:24–34*

When you read these pages you may think, 'Does the Bible really say that?' The best thing you can do is to find out for yourself! Most of the pages have a Bible Search so that you can look up the verses in your own Bible.

ANY QUESTIONS

These questions help you examine text more closely, and to think about some of the Bible's teachings.

THE BIBLE
There are 66 books in the Bible. This may seem like a lot of pages, but there is an easy system for finding your way around:

- Each Bible book is split up into chapters, and each chapter has a number. Exodus 1 means the first chapter of the Book of Exodus. Usually these numbers are set at the top of each page in your Bible.
- Each chapter is split up into short sections of one or two lines. These are called verses. Verses also have numbers. The verse numbers are the small numbers on each page. So Exodus 1:12 means verse 12 of chapter 1 of the Book of Exodus.

On many pages you will see the words 'See also' or 'To find out more'. By turning to the suggested pages, you can follow a story or a subject through the book. For example, read about Ghosts and demons, then turn to Superstition and magic, and then to Deuteronomy, and so on.

BC refers to all the years before Jesus was born: 500 BC means 500 years before Jesus was born. AD refers to all the years after Jesus was born.
All the dates of events in the Old Testament are 'BC'; all the dates in the New Testament are 'AD'.

4

Balaam's donkey stops when it sees the angel

ANGELS GOD'S MESSENGERS

The word angel comes from a Greek word meaning messenger. As far as we can tell, angels don't have wings! The angels who appeared in Jesus' tomb on Easter Sunday wore dazzling white clothes.

WHAT DO ANGELS DO?

- They pass on God's messages.
- They help God's people.
- They punish God's enemies.
- They explain God's plans.

DIFFERENT ANGELS

Gabriel
The angel Gabriel told Mary that Jesus was going to be born.

Michael
The archangel, or chief of the angels, was Michael. He was the commander-in-chief of God's army of angels.

Angels wore dazzling white clothes

Satan
Satan was an angel who decided to turn against God.

The angel of the Lord
This was the name given to an angel who often seemed to represent God himself. The angel of the Lord spoke to Moses out of a burning bush.

Guardian angels
Jesus said that children have their own angels.

TRAVELLERS

Often angels were disguised as ordinary people. Abraham did not know that the three visitors, who came to tell him that he and his wife Sarah would have a baby, were angels.

BALAAM AND THE INVISIBLE ANGEL

Balaam was a fortune-teller. The king of the Moabites was frightened of the Israelites and sent for Balaam. He wanted him to put a curse on the Israelites so that the Moabites would be able to defeat them in battle.

When Balaam set off on his donkey, to travel to the king, the donkey stopped in the road. Balaam was furious. But the donkey had seen an angel holding a sword, blocking their way. Balaam couldn't see the angel, and beat the donkey. Then God made Balaam able to see the angel too. The angel said that the donkey had saved Balaam's life, because if it had continued on its way, the angel would have killed Balaam.

Bible Search

- Climbing a staircase: *Genesis 28:12*
- Cooking a meal: *1 Kings 19:5–7*
- In chariots of fire: *2 Kings 6:15–17*
- Passing on a battle plan: *Joshua 5:13–6:5*
- Helping Jesus: *Mark 1:13*

Guardian angels look after children

ANGER GOOD AND BAD

Jesus upsets the traders' tables at the Temple

Anger is a strong feeling that rises up inside us when something bad happens. Sometimes it's good to be angry. The Old Testament prophets were angry when the people disobeyed God, and so was Jesus.

It's wrong to be angry just because we can't get what we want, or if we want to hurt the person who made us angry.

Feeling angry

WHEN ANGER IS GOOD

Some children came to see Jesus, but the disciples tried to turn them away. Jesus was angry. 'Let the children come to me,' he said. We should be angry when we see innocent people treated unfairly, or when people get away with doing wrong.

USING ANGER

One day, Jesus went into the Temple, and saw that God's house of prayer had been turned into a market. He was very angry, and turned over the traders' tables and drove out the animals. Jesus used his anger to change things.

When we see something that is wrong, we too can try to put it right.

CALM DOWN

What should we do when someone is angry with us? The Bible gives some guidelines:
- Listen carefully. (See James 1:19.)
- Do something kind. (See Romans 12:20.)
- Reply gently. (See Proverbs 15:1.)
- Talk it over with other people. (See Matthew 18:15.)

Paul wrote: 'Get rid of all bitterness and anger...be kind and tender-hearted to one another, and forgive one another as God has forgiven you...'

WHEN ANGER IS WRONG

Villagers send Jesus and the disciples away

Jesus sent his friends to a village in Samaria. 'We don't want you here,' the villagers said. James and John were angry. 'Should we call fire down from heaven to kill these people?' they asked. But Jesus rebuked them, and said he had come to save people, not destroy them. Then he went to another town.

It's important to know how to deal with anger, in ourselves and in other people.

Bible Search
- David gets angry: 1 Samuel 25:1–13
- Abigail calms David: 1 Samuel 25: 14–35
- Jesus and children: Mark 10:13–16
- Fire from heaven: Luke 9:51–59

6

ANIMALS CARING FOR

Many animals suffer at the hands of humans, often as the result of our greed. This is directly opposite to the teaching of the Bible.

Egg-laying hens are reared in cages, where they can't move. Animals are experimented on, to test cosmetics or household cleaners.

Bible Search

- Animals in need: **Deuteronomy 22:1–4**
- Wild animals: **Leviticus 25:7**
- Balaam's donkey: **Numbers 22:21–33**
- New world: **Isaiah 11:6–9**

ANY QUESTIONS

1 Why did God make Balaam's donkey able to speak?
2 What is unusual about a wolf living with a lamb?

BIBLE TEACHING

Jesus said that not even the tiniest sparrow died without God knowing about it. The Bible includes some rules which told people how to treat their animals:

- If a donkey falls down under its load, help it up, even if the donkey belongs to your enemy.
- Poor people and wild animals should be allowed to help themselves to food from fields and orchards.

AN ANGEL AND A DONKEY

Balaam was riding along the road on his donkey. Suddenly, an angel with a flaming sword appeared in front of him, blocking the way. Balaam could not see him, but his donkey could, and turned off the road into a field. Balaam beat the donkey in annoyance.

Twice more the angel appeared in the donkey's path, and the donkey stopped. Each time, Balaam beat it.

Then God made the donkey able to speak, and it asked Balaam: 'What have I done to you? Why have you hit me?' Balaam replied furiously, 'Because you disobeyed me.'

Finally, God made Balaam able to see the angel. The angel told Balaam that the donkey had saved his life by moving out of the way.

The Bible said that a donkey must be helped if it fell

THE FUTURE

'The wolf will live with the lamb...'

The Bible pictures God's new world as a place where human beings and animals will live peacefully together.

'The leopard will lie down with the goat...'

The Bible says: 'The wolf will live with the lamb, the leopard will lie down with the goat, the calf and the lion and the yearling together; and a little child will lead them.'

BAPTISM ENTERING THE CHRISTIAN FAITH

The word baptism comes from a Greek word meaning to dip (in water). When you are baptized, water is put on your body as a sign to show you are made clean from sin. Before Jesus went back to heaven, he told his disciples, 'Go and make disciples of all nations, baptizing them in the name of the Father and of the Son and of the Holy Spirit…'

Christians from all over the world

PETER'S SERMON

The apostle Peter's punchline, at the end of his first sermon, was 'Repent (turn away from your sins) and be baptized, every one of you… in the name of Jesus Christ for the forgiveness of your sins.' Three thousand people became followers of Jesus that day, and were baptized.

A PRISON OFFICER

Paul and Silas had been beaten and thrown in prison for teaching Christianity. One day, there was an earthquake, and the prison doors flew open. But Paul and Silas didn't try to escape. The prison officer was so impressed with their courage that he asked if he could be a Christian. That night, he and all his family were baptized.

Bible Search

- Bronze basin: *Exodus 30:17–21*
- Jesus' words: *Matthew 28:19–20*
- Peter's first sermon: *Acts 2:14–41*
- In prison: *Acts 16:16–34*

After listening to Peter's sermon, many people wanted to be baptized

BAPTISM TODAY

Some people are baptized as babies. They have a few drops of water dabbed on their foreheads from a font (often a stone basin) in the church. Their parents make promises to God for them. When the baby has grown up, he or she makes the promises for him or herself. This second service is often called confirmation.

A baptism

ADULT BAPTISM

Some people say that baptism only makes sense if the person baptized understands what is happening, and so there is no point in being baptized as a baby. So instead, they often hold a church service to say thank you to God when a baby is born. Baptism only takes place later on, when a person has decided to follow Jesus.

In some churches, during an adult's baptism, the person's whole body is ducked beneath the water.

CHRISTIAN LIFE: STARTING

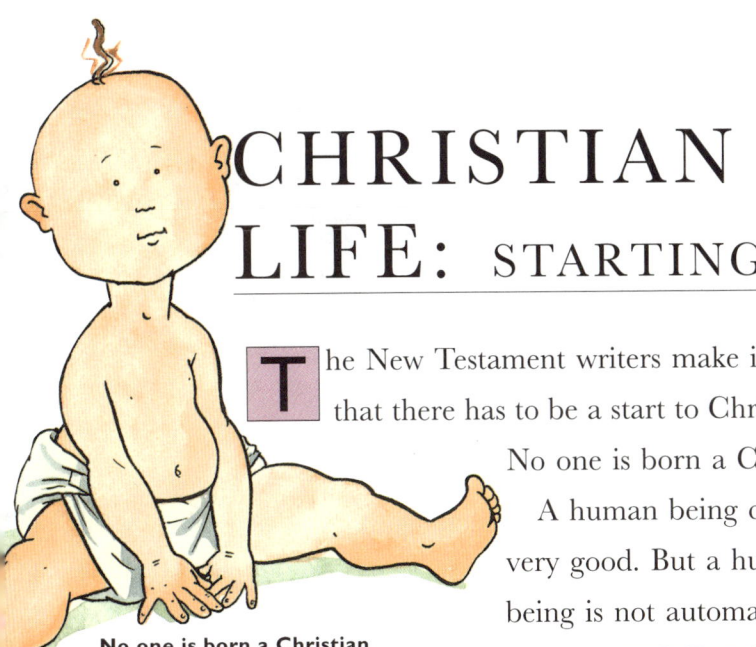

No one is born a Christian

The New Testament writers make it clear that there has to be a start to Christian life. No one is born a Christian. A human being can be very good. But a human being is not automatically a child of God. For that to happen, a new type of life is needed. And that new life is given, as a gift, when someone trusts Jesus.

BORN AGAIN

John wrote: 'To all who receive him (Jesus), to those who believed in his name, he gave the right to become children of God…' And Jesus said, 'No one can enter the kingdom of God unless he is born again…the Spirit gives birth to the Spirit.'

FINDING THE WAY

It may happen in this way. Let's look at what happens to a boy called Michael.
- Michael believes Jesus is the son of God, who died to set him free.
- Michael sees that compared with Jesus, things in his life are wrong, pointless, empty, or second-rate.
- Michael tells Jesus he is sorry. He asks Jesus to be his friend, and to take charge of his life. From now on he is 'under new management'.

Bible Search
- A promise: **John 6:37**
- New birth: **John 1:12; 3:3–6**
- Life at its best: **John 10:10**
- Zacchaeus: **Luke 19:8–9**
- Trusting: **Ephesians 2:8–9**

Michael

A TURN-AROUND

Sometimes when people become Christians, we say they have converted to Christianity. It happens in different ways:

- Paul saw Jesus in a blinding light on the road to Damascus, and stopped attacking Christians.
- Zacchaeus had a meal with Jesus, and stopped stealing money.

Zacchaeus and Jesus

- Timothy learned about Jesus when he was little.

Some people will tell you the exact hour they became Christians. Some people cannot remember when or how the change came. This doesn't matter. What is important is that they can say, 'Now I trust Jesus.' Jesus said, 'Whoever comes to me I will never turn away.'

CHRISTIAN LIFE: LIVING

Religion was a burden to most people in the time of Jesus. It was made up of hundreds of rules. That's why Jesus said, 'Come to me, all you who are weary… and I will give you rest… for my burden is light.'

The way of life Jesus offers is not an easy option. But Jesus helps us. 'The load with my help is light,' he said.

With Jesus your load is lightened

WHAT JESUS WANTS

Jesus said to his followers, 'If anyone would follow me, he must deny himself and take up his cross and follow me.' This means doing what Jesus wants, not what we want.

Jesus said, 'Suppose a man wants to build a watchtower. First of all he works out the cost. If he starts to build, but has to give up because he runs out of money, everyone will make fun of him. In the same way, think before you decide to follow me. It's all or nothing. Are you ready for that?'

A man plans to build a watchtower

LIVING

How should a Christian live? Here are some pointers:

- Praying. This is how we keep in touch with Jesus.

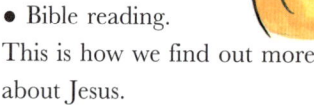

- Bible reading. This is how we find out more about Jesus.

- Loving. Christians are meant to live in the love of God, wanting God's best for other people.

- Keeping going. Sometimes, we fail Jesus. We have to pick ourselves up, say sorry and keep on going (see the page on Temptation).

- Witnessing. (See next page.)

JESUS WITH ME

Question: How can Jesus be with me? I can't see him!
Answer: The Holy Spirit is the power, love and presence of Jesus with us.

BELONGING

Christians belong to God's family. They can help each other. Above all, God has promised to take care of his children, who belong to his kingdom. (See the pages on Kingdom of God and Church.)

Bible Search

- Rest: *Matthew 11:28–29*
- A death blow: *Mark 8:34–35*
- A watchtower: *Luke 14:28–33*
- The Spirit of Jesus: *Galatians 5:25; John 16:7*

CHRISTIAN LIFE:
WITNESSING

One of the last things Jesus said to his friends was this: 'You will receive power when the Holy Spirit comes on you; and you will be my witnesses in Jerusalem… and to the ends of the Earth.' Jesus still wants Christians to be his witnesses. With the help of the Spirit of Jesus, we can let our friends see the love of Jesus.

THE REASON WHY…

This is how Peter put it: 'But you are…a people belonging to God that you may declare the praises of him who called you out of darkness into his marvellous light.'

A LAMP

Jesus said, 'You are the light of the world.' No one lights a lamp and then hides it. 'In the same way,' Jesus said, 'let your light shine before men, that they may see your good deeds and praise your father in heaven.'

Bible Search

- Witnesses: *Acts 1:8*
- Praising: *1 Peter 2:9*
- A lamp: *Matthew 5:14–16*
- Don't be ashamed: *Luke 9:26*
- Caring: *Luke 10:25–37*
- Forgiving: *Matthew 6:12*

WITNESSING

How do Christians give witness to Jesus? Here are some ideas:
- By speaking

This doesn't mean we have to go around preaching to people! But sometimes our friends may ask us questions about God, and we can try to answer them. Or we can talk to other Christians about the way Jesus has helped us. Sometimes, it might mean standing up for Jesus when he is laughed at. Jesus said, 'Don't be ashamed of me.'

We can say how Jesus has helped us

We can stand up for Jesus

- By caring

- By fighting wrong things

- By forgiving

CHURCH A FAMILY

'The Church' means all the people, all over the world, who are followers of Jesus Christ. The word 'church' today also describes the building where Christians meet. In the New Testament, the word 'church' means either a group of Christians in one place, or the complete number of believers.

A FAMILY

The Church is often called 'a family'. John wrote that each person who believes in Jesus becomes a child of God. God is their father, and other Christians are brothers and sisters. This stresses the loving care all Christians should have for each other.

A BODY

Paul (then called Saul) was attacking Christians. Then he saw a great light in the sky and he heard Jesus say, 'Why do you attack me?' So Paul understood that Jesus and Christians are closely united. Paul compared Christianity to a body. Jesus was the head, and each Christian was a part of the body. Every single Christian has a different job to do in the Church, just as a hand, a foot and an eye have different jobs to do in a body.

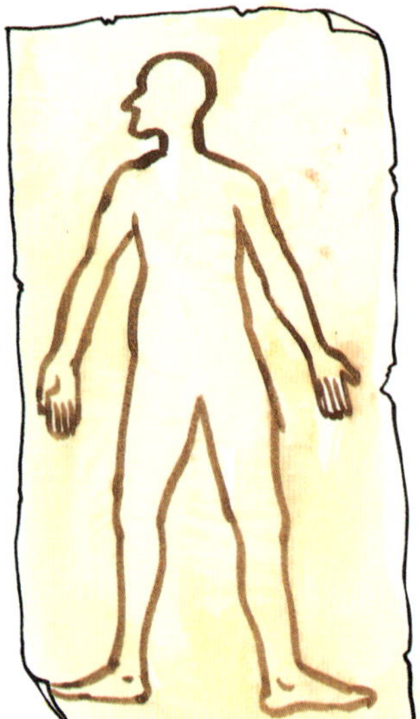

If you catch flu, your whole body aches. When Christians are in trouble, Jesus (the head) and fellow Christians (the rest of the body) often feel the pain too and try to help.

Feeling ill

Bible Search
- The body, and its gifts:
**Romans 12:1–8;
1 Corinthians 12;
1 Peter 4:10–11;
Ephesians 4:1–16**

GIFTS

The Holy Spirit gives abilities to Christians so that they can help one another to know God better, and to show God's love in the world. In your church group, for example, you might find that each person is good at different things:

- Thinking up new ideas.

Thinking up new ideas

- Helping others to understand the Bible.
- Getting things done.
- Listening.
- Talking about Jesus.

All these, and more, are gifts of the Holy Spirit. No one has every gift! Each one is important.

Getting things done

12

God made us all different

CHURCH ONE AND MANY

Bible Search

- Love:
  1 Corinthians 8:1–2
- Fan clubs:
  1 Corinthians 1:10–17; 3:1–16
- Jesus' prayer:
  John 17:20–23

The poet R. L. Stevenson once wrote:

*'The world is so full of a number of things
I'm sure we should all be as happy as kings.'*

God has made us all different. We should be glad about this.

DIFFERENCES

Some Christians like to worship God in a majestic cathedral. Others prefer a small, friendly group in someone's house. Such differences only become a problem when Christians start criticising each other, and saying their group is better than another.

Paul wrote that a Christian should not claim to know better than another Christian. He said, 'Knowledge puffs up, but love builds up. The man who thinks he knows something does not yet…But the man who loves God is known by God.'

People worship God in different places

PEOPLE

Christians should not be rivals

Some Christians are very impressed by a certain preacher, and start saying he or she is better than the others.

This happened in Corinth. Paul wrote: 'I appeal to you, brothers, that there may be no divisions among you…One of you says, "I follow Paul", another, "I follow Apollos", another, "I follow Cephas"…' Paul said this was wrong, as all the men were servants of God, each with his own gifts and work. They were not rivals.

DOCTRINE

'Doctrine' means Christian teaching. Some Christians break away from other Christians, because they disagree about the way they understand the teaching of the Bible.

After his last supper, Jesus prayed for all the people who would one day believe in him. He said, 'May they be brought to complete unity, that the world may know you have sent me…' When Christians fight and argue, it gives non-Christians a bad idea of Christianity.

Christians fighting and arguing

TAIZÉ

At Taizé, a little village in the hills of Burgundy in France, thousands of Christians from all over the world meet together to pray, talk and study the Bible. All kinds of people, from bishops and nuns, to students and old people, from every kind of church, find there are no barriers between them.

13

CREATION AND EVOLUTION

Tiny living cells

Christians discuss how the world was created

Evolution is another way of looking at how the world was created. It is an idea that means that over billions of years we have evolved from tiny cells into human beings. Over the centuries, there have been many theories about how people were created.

The theory of evolution was developed in the last century by a man called Charles Darwin. Some Christians accept this idea and say that God used evolution to make the world, but others disagree. So Christians have many discussions about their different views.

DIFFERENT VIEWS

- View One.
Some Christians say the theory of evolution goes against the teaching of the book of Genesis. They say that as the Bible does not tell lies, evolution must be a lie.
- View Two.
Other people say evolution proves that there is no God. It shows that the world came about by chance and that people are just like animals.
- View Three.
Some Christians believe that people have misunderstood Genesis chapter one. They say that Genesis is not a science textbook. It is more like a poetry book. Science can explain how the world was made. Genesis says who made the world. These Christians say that the seven days in which God created the world were not like our kind of days – they were very long periods of time, lasting billions of years.

THEORY OF EVOLUTION

The theory of evolution says that this is how living creatures developed. The first life on Earth was tiny living cells in the sea. As these cells reproduced, small changes appeared. All plants, animals and people came from these first cells. Over billions of years, they developed in different ways into different things.

FINDING OUT

If you pulled a TV to pieces, you might be able to find out how it works, but you will not find the man who made the TV inside it! This is a little like the way in which a scientist examines the world.

The scientist can try to find out how the world works. But he or she won't meet God by doing this. So the theory of evolution does not prove or disprove anything about God. You find God in a different way.

How does a TV work?

14

CREED
WHAT A CHRISTIAN BELIEVES

A creed is a statement of what someone believes. One of the earliest Christian creeds was: 'Jesus is Lord'. Sometimes false teachers spread strange ideas about Jesus. So Christians met together to work out creeds, or statements of the Christian faith.

Christians meet to work out a creed

Bible Search

- Paul: **Romans 10:9**
- Passing on what you know: **2 Timothy 1:13; 2:2**
- Jesus is Lord: **Acts 2:36**

THE APOSTLES' CREED

This probably wasn't written by the apostles, but it does date back to the very early days of the Church, perhaps to the year AD 150. It is likely that the Apostles' Creed is a statement of the first Christians' beliefs.

The creed begins, 'I believe in…' It is about the facts that Christians believe, but also about the trust they feel in God.

The Apostles' Creed

I believe in God, the Father almighty, creator of heaven and Earth,

I believe in Jesus Christ, his only Son, our Lord
He was conceived by the power of the Holy Spirit
and born of the Virgin Mary.
He suffered under Pontius Pilate, was crucified, died, and was buried.
He descended to the dead.
On the third day he rose again.
He ascended into heaven, and is seated at the right hand of the Father.
He will come again to judge the living and the dead.

I believe in the Holy Spirit;
the holy Catholic Church,
the communion of saints,
the forgiveness of sins,
the resurrection of the body,
and the life everlasting.

WORD FOR WORD

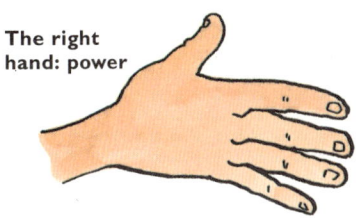
The right hand: power

These are the meanings of some of the words in the Apostles' Creed.
- Right hand: power
- Catholic: world-wide
- Communion: sharing in friendship
- Saints: all Christians

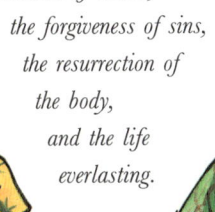

A creed unites Christians

15

DEATH AND KILLING

When, if ever, is it right to kill another person? This is an age-old question, but medical technology also raises some new problems. It is possible to find guidelines in the Bible, but Christians sometimes reach opposite conclusions from these. In that case, Christians must respect another person's sincerely-held opinion.

SOME PROBLEMS

- Should murderers be killed?

The death sentence?

- Do I have the right to end my own life?

Suicide?

- Should a foetus be aborted?
- If someone is kept alive in a hospital by a machine, when should that machine be turned off?

Should a machine be turned off?

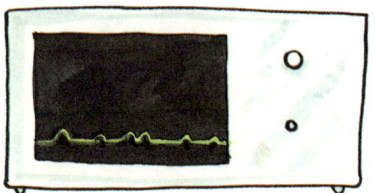

- Is war ever right?
- Should a dying person be helped to die?

BIBLE GUIDELINES

- Life is a gift from God, and should be treated with reverence.
- God is in control of life. Human beings should obey God's laws.
- Jesus gave us a deeper understanding of many Old Testament laws. He taught that love is the rule in life, not revenge.
- Weak people are to be protected.
- Death is part of someone's life; it is not the end.
- Jesus said to Peter, 'Put your sword back in its place. All who draw the sword will die by the sword.'

'Put your sword away.'

Bible Search

- People reflect God's nature: **Genesis 1:27**
- Do not murder: **Matthew 5:21**
- Strength from God: **Philippians 4:13**
- Put back your sword: **Matthew 26:52**

ABORTION

Abortion is an operation to terminate a woman's pregnancy at a very early stage, when the baby is still a tiny foetus. Abortion is always a very difficult decision.

Some Christians think that the Biblical guideline of protecting the weak, should always be applied here. Others believe that abortion is sometimes necessary, for example if the mother's life is in danger, or if the baby would be severely handicapped.

THE HOSPICE MOVEMENT

In recent years, the hospice movement has grown. In a hospice, people who are terminally ill spend their last days being cared for in gentle and loving way

Care in a hospice

THE SAMARITANS

In 1953, Chad Varah, a clergyman, invited anyone who was considering suicide to phone him. This idea grew into an organization called the Samaritans. Today the Samaritans receive over two million calls a year.

Calling the Samaritans

DEVIL THE ENEMY OF CHRISTIANITY

The Devil, or Satan, is the centre-point of evil in the world. After Jesus was baptized, he went off by himself into the desert. There he was tempted by the Devil. But Jesus didn't give in. The Devil doesn't have God's power. When Jesus was alive, he always conquered the Devil.

Jesus is tempted by the Devil

A BAD ANGEL

No one knows where the Devil came from. But the Bible seems to suggest that he was an angel who became jealous of God. He was thrown out of heaven, and now tries to get revenge.

A DEADLY ENEMY

The Devil is the enemy of Christianity:
- The Devil masterminded the death of Jesus.
- The Devil stops people believing in Jesus. 'The god of this age has blinded the minds of unbelievers,' said Paul.
- The Devil wants to destroy Christians. Peter wrote: 'Your enemy the Devil prowls around like a roaring lion looking for someone to devour.'

Bible Search

- The world: *John 15:18–19; 17:15*
- Armour: *Ephesians 6:10–18*
- Resist: *James 4:7*
- Jesus with us: *1 John 4:4*

- The Devil has many disguises. Jesus called the Devil 'the father of lies'. Paul tells us that the Devil could change himself to look like an angel of light!
- One of the Devil's main tricks is to tempt people to do wrong, by making it seem right (see the page on Temptation).

Peter compared the Devil to a prowling lion

THE WORLD

The word 'world' had another meaning in the Bible: it described all the people and organizations that didn't obey God. Jesus called the Devil the 'prince of the world'.

One day on the far shore of the Sea of Galilee, Jesus met a madman. The madman was so strong that he smashed the chains people put on him. He felt he had been taken over by evil spirits. Jesus healed him and said, 'The prince of this world has no hold on me.'

The madman broke the chains that were holding him

The Devil thought he had won when Jesus died. He didn't expect Jesus to rise again! Paul wrote that Jesus triumphed over the Devil by the cross.

Jesus rose from the dead

17

DRUGS AND ADDICTIONS

A drug is a substance which alters the chemistry of the body. Some drugs take away pain; others give a feeling of happiness. The word drug has come to be used for anything that gives people a 'high'. People who can't live without a drug are addicted to it.

Tea, coffee and cigarettes are all legal drugs

FOOD

Eating problems

These days many people can't control their eating. Some people eat far too much; other people starve themselves.

The Devil tempted Jesus to use his powers to get food when he was in the wilderness. Jesus said to the Devil: 'Man should not live on bread alone, but on every word that comes from the mouth of God.' He meant that food should not control our lives.

HOPE

People can be cured from addictions with the help of doctors and friends. Many find they are helped by prayer and the friendship of Jesus. Jesus said, 'I have come that they may have life, and have it to the full.'

Paul described our bodies as a temple which we should take care of. He wrote: 'Don't you know that you yourselves are God's temple, and that God's Spirit lives in you.'

DRUGS

Some drugs are legal, such as alcohol, coffee and cigarettes.

Alcohol is not harmful if we don't drink too much of it. Even Jesus drank wine. However, some people can't control their drinking and become alcoholics. Some Christians don't drink at all, to show that life can be lived without alcohol!

Cigarettes are another common drug, but they are dangerous to health.

The government has banned many harmful drugs. Some people still take them, perhaps to act big or to escape problems. But when the drug wears off, the problem is still there.

After the drug has worn off

GAMBLING

Cards and dice are used for gambling

Some people are addicted to the excitement of gambling. Many Christians say that money is a gift from God and should be put to good use, not gambled in the hope of getting more back.

Bible Search

- Paul's advice: *Timothy 5:23*
- Temple: *1 Corinthians 3:16,17*
- Jesus: *Matthew 4:4; John 10:10*
- Setting an example: *1 Corinthians 8:13*

END OF THE WORLD

How will the world end? A large meteor could come crashing into our planet. Or we could blow ourselves up. But Christian teaching is that it will not happen by chance: the end of the world is in God's control.

Jesus said the end of the world would be unexpected, like a thief in the night. 'Be ready for my coming at any time!' Jesus said.

WHEN?

The Old Testament teachers promised that God would put an end to the evil in the world. The first step was Jesus' birth in Bethlehem, and the final step will be the end of the world. Bible teaching on this subject is often difficult to understand.

Jesus said that only God knew when the end of the world would be. It could be tomorrow, or in thousands of years' time. We should not waste our time trying to work out when it will be.

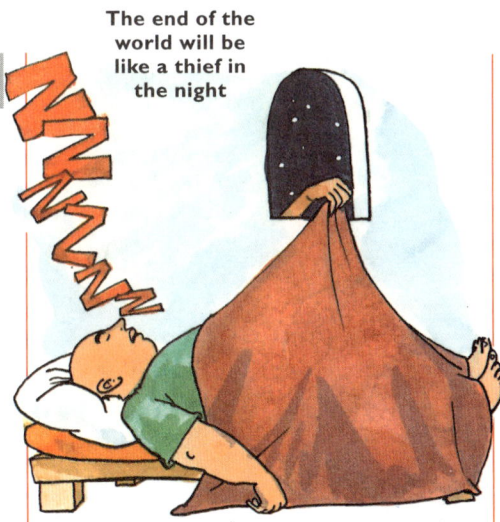

The end of the world will be like a thief in the night

SECOND COMING

The Bible says that when the world ends, Jesus will come again, and this time the whole world will know about him. He will come as a great king, with all his angels.

Dead people are in eternity with Jesus. But when the world ends, they will come back to life, with new bodies. The Bible does not say what these new bodies will be like. Paul compared them to a plant and a seed. A plant, although it comes from a seed, does not look like a seed.

JUDGMENT DAY

The Bible says that at the end of the world, everybody will be judged.

Then God will make a new Earth. There will be no more suffering of any kind.

Everybody will be judged

Working out when the end of the world will come

- Be ready: *Mark 13:32–36*
- Judgment: *Matthew 25:31–46*
- New world: *Revelation 21:1–5*
- Jesus speaks to everyone: *Romans 2:12–16*

Bible Search

FAITH A STRONG BELIEF

A Roman soldier asks Jesus for help

Faith is deciding that Jesus is God and that he is as real as you are, and then relying on God's promises and living his way. Believing in God, but not showing it by your actions, is not faith. 'Even the demons believe,' said James. Faith means keeping going when everything is difficult.

Three strangers visit Abraham

ABRAHAM

One day in the desert, three strangers came to Abraham. They were angels. 'You will have a son,' God said. Abraham and his wife were very old, but that didn't stop Abraham trusting God's promise. It was a great example of faith.

A WAY OF LIFE

God gave Jesus to be our friend. He asks us to trust Jesus.
- By trusting Jesus we become God's true children.
- By trusting that Jesus died on the cross to take the punishment for our sins, we receive forgiveness.
- In daily life, trusting that Jesus keeps his promises, helps us to see his power at work.

Faith is deciding to trust and obey Jesus without proof that he loves us and that he is able to help us. Sometimes faith means keeping going when there seems no reason, and everything is black and difficult.

Jesus and his friends

A SOLDIER

'Please heal my servant,' said a soldier to Jesus. 'I'll come with you,' said Jesus. The soldier said, 'I'm not good enough for you to come to my house. I know that if you give the command, my servant will be healed.' 'This Roman soldier has more faith than anyone I've found,' said Jesus. And he healed the servant.

FAITH WORKS

'We've seen Jesus. He's alive again!' said Jesus' friends to Thomas. 'It's impossible. I don't believe you,' said Thomas. 'I'll only believe if I can see him and touch him for myself.'

Jesus came to Thomas. 'Look at me,' he said. 'Stop doubting and believe. Those who believe without seeing me will be truly happy.'

On another occasion, a sick woman touched Jesus' cloak. 'Daughter, your faith has healed you. Go in peace and be freed from your suffering,' said Jesus.

- Abraham: **Romans 4:18–25**
- God's promise: **John 3:16–19**
- Heroes and heroines of faith: **Hebrews 11**
- A sick woman: **Mark 5:24–34**

FAME
AND AMBITION

If someone asks you, 'What do you want to be when you're grown up?', you might reply, 'I want to be famous and have lots of money.'

We should always try and make the most of our abilities. But if our only aim in life is to get to the top, and if we look down on people who don't do so well, then we've lost sight of Jesus.

Wanting to be rich and famous

WELL DONE

Jesus told a story about three servants who were given sums of money by their master. Two of the men increased the money by buying and selling. Their master was very pleased with them. But the third servant buried his money in the ground. The master was angry at the servant's stupidity. Jesus was saying that the most important thing is to do what God wants. That makes us 'famous' in his eyes, whatever our position in the world.

The servant who buried the money

DON'T SHOW OFF

Trying to sit next to the host

At parties, guests often tried to show how important or famous they were by choosing the best seats either side of the host.

Jesus said, 'Don't sit down in the place of honour, somebody more important than you may have been invited. Sit lower down the table, and your host may ask you to move further up. Then everyone will see the respect in which you're held.'

ANY QUESTIONS
1 What sort of ambitions is it good to have?
2 Is it right to want to be famous?

JAMES AND JOHN

Jesus told the disciples that he would be killed and then rise again. James and John asked if they could sit on his right and left (the best seats) when Jesus was brought back to life. Jesus said, 'Rulers love to show their power over people… but if one of you wants to become great, then he must serve the others like a servant…'

AMBITION

It is wrong to be ambitious if our aim is just to increase our fame or wealth. Jeremiah said to his servant: 'Should you seek great things for yourself? Seek them not.' But Paul's ambitions were good: to preach the gospel of Jesus in new places, and to know Jesus.

Bible Search

- James and John: *Mark 10:35–45*
- The best seats: *Luke 14:7–10*
- Using ability: *Luke 19:11–28*
- Good ambition: *Romans 15:20; Philippians 3:10–11*

FAMILIES TODAY

Every family is different

The traditional idea of a family is two parents and a child or children, plus other relations such as grandparents, aunts, uncles and cousins. But every family is different. There are many families with just one parent; other families have grown to include half-sisters, half-brothers and stepmother or stepfather. These large families remind us of the large families of Bible times.

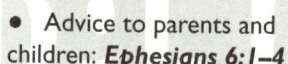

Some families have one parent

A GIFT

Family rows

Families are God's gift, but there are often problems within families.

There were family problems in Bible times too; for example Joseph's brothers sold him to be a slave, and King David's son, Absalom, plotted to drive his father from the palace.

PARENTS AND CHILDREN

The apostle Paul wrote: 'Do not make your children angry. But raise them with the training and teaching of the Lord.'

Parents who love their children try to make sure they grow up in the right way. The Book of Proverbs says: 'The Lord corrects those he loves, just as a father corrects the child that he likes.'

The fifth commandment says, 'Honour (respect) your father and mother.' Paul wrote: 'Children obey your parents the way the Lord wants. This is the right thing to do.'

Paul said, 'A believer should take care of his own relatives, especially his own family.' When Jesus was dying on the cross, he told his friend John to look after Mary, his mother.

Children should obey their parents

Bible Search

- Advice to parents and children: *Ephesians 6:1–4*
- Jesus: *Matthew 12:46–49*
- Caring for the elderly: *1 Timothy 5:4; 8*
- Punishing children: *Proverbs 3:12*

JESUS

Jesus said, 'Whoever does the will of my father in heaven is my brother and sister and mother.' The term 'family' also describes a group of people who live together because they love God and obey him. Many nuns and monks consider themselves to be a family.

22

Feeling guilty

FORGIVENESS
FROM GOD

Many people feel guilty because of wrong things they've done. For these people, the Christian message is good news. God accepts people exactly as they are. He loves them, forgives them, and then gives them the power to change.

Forgiveness is God's gift, but we have to want it and accept it.

Bible Search

- Falling short: *Romans 3:23*
- Wiping out debts: *Colossians 2:13–14*
- The gift: *Ephesians 2:4; 5; 8*
- Jesus: *1 Peter 2:24*

SIN

When we do something wrong, we are doing wrong against God. The word for this is sin. Sin is a rebellion against God, when we have not followed his laws and gone our own way. The story of Adam and Eve is the story of the first sin.

An archer may shoot an arrow which falls short of the target. In the Bible, sin is sometimes described as 'missing the mark', falling short of God's standard.

Missing the mark

FORGIVENESS

Sometimes sin is pictured as a list of wrong things, rather like an 'I Owe You', that we need to pay up. Paul said, 'He forgives us all our sins, and has cancelled the written code (wiped out the list of debts).'

Forgiveness is not easy. God is completely good, right and fair. He can't just excuse wrong. The Bible says that the punishment for sin is 'death', meaning being cut off from God.

Wiping out debts

JESUS

Jesus died on the cross as punishment for our sins. Peter wrote: 'He himself bore our sins in his body on the tree… by his wounds you have been healed.'

A RUNAWAY SON

Jesus told a story about a son who took his share of his father's money and left home. He had a great time, until he ran out of money, and had to take a job looking after pigs. Then he saw what a fool he'd been, and set off home. His father rushed to meet him. The son said, 'Dad, I've sinned against God and against you…' His father threw a party to celebrate his return. It is a picture of how God accepts people who are really sorry.

The son enjoys himself

The son returns

FORGIVENESS
FORGIVING ONE ANOTHER

When someone upsets or hurts us we want to hit back. Sometimes, if we can't hurt the person who hurt us, we hurt someone else. Some people hold on to their grudges for years. They want to get their own back; they want revenge. For many people, forgiveness only begins to be possible when they think about Jesus.

Sometim[es]
we wa[nt]
rever[ge]

JESUS

Jesus did no wrong at all. Yet his enemies made him suffer death by slow torture. He took the pain, horror and hatred into himself, and changed it into love. On the cross he said, 'Father, forgive them, they don't know what they are doing.'

Jesus suffered death by slow torture

LAW-BREAKERS

Two of God's commandments are, 'Love God with your whole self' and 'Love your neighbour as you love yourself.' We often break these laws, yet God forgives us. So we should forgive other people. Paul wrote: 'Be kind and compassionate to one another, forgiving each other, just as in Christ, God forgave you.'

A STORY

Jesus told a story about a servant who owed his king a huge amount of money. 'Sell him, his family, and his house,' said the king.

The servant begged the king to give him chance to pay back the money, and the king felt sorry for him and wiped out the debt.

The servant went away and found someone to whom he had lent a little money. 'Pay up or else,' said the servant. 'I'm sorry, I can't,' the man said. So the servant had the man thrown into prison.

The king was furious when he found out. The servant was punished until he had paid every last penny.

The servant is punished

FORGIVE AND FORGET

Jesus said, 'If you forgive men when they sin against you, your heavenly Father will also forgive you. But if you do not forgive men their sins, your Father will not forgive you.' Forgiving doesn't just mean saying, 'I forgive you.' It means forgetting all about the wrong, and wiping it out of your mind.

Forgiving each other

Bible Search

- Wages of sin: *Romans 3:20*
- Unforgiving servant: *Matthew 18:21–35*
- Forgiving others: *Matthew 6:12, 14–15*

FREEDOM
THROUGH JESUS

'I am with you and I will rescue you,' said God to Jeremiah. God sets his people free. This is seen throughout the Bible, starting with God's rescue of the Israelite slaves from Egypt. When Jesus began his work, he said, 'The Spirit of the Lord… has sent me to proclaim freedom for the captives.'

FREEDOM

There are different sorts of freedom. There is the freedom to choose one thing instead of another. Children may often have a more limited freedom to choose, because parents decide for them!

There is also inner freedom: being free from fear, worry, guilt, bad habits, and wrong thoughts. This is the freedom which Jesus came to give to everyone through Christianity.

A CRIPPLED WOMAN

In the synagogue one Sabbath, Jesus saw a woman who couldn't stand up straight. Jesus said to her, 'You are set free from your illness.' The Pharisees grumbled that Jesus was working on the Sabbath. But Jesus said, 'Satan has tied up this woman for eighteen years. Shouldn't I set her free?'

Jesus heals a crippled woman

Parents often make choices for their children

Bible Search
- The Spirit: *2 Corinthians 3:17; Galatians 5:16–18*
- Bad habits: *Romans 7:18–19; 8:2–4*
- What freedom is for: *Galatians 5:13*
- Slave to sin: *John 8:31–36*

RULES

Burdened by rules

The Jews thought that if they worked very hard to keep all God's laws, they would go to heaven. They felt they had to earn God's love. But Jesus showed that going to heaven was a gift, because no one lives perfectly and deserves heaven.

Paul said, 'It is for freedom Christ has set us free…do not be burdened again by a yoke of slavery.' By 'yoke' he meant religious laws and rules devised by people.

WHAT FREEDOM IS FOR

Does Jesus set us free to do whatever we like? The answer is 'no'. People are made to serve, just as birds are made to fly. Jesus set us free to serve God and each another.

Paul wrote that the Holy Spirit helped Christians to live in freedom.

We are all lonely sometimes

FRIENDSHIP
CARING AND SHARING

Human beings need friends. This is how God made us. Adam, the first man, was alone and lonely. But then God made Eve so that she could be a friend for Adam.

The Book of Proverbs has some wise words about friends: 'A friend loves at all times.' Most people find that at some time in their life they are lonely. Whatever the reason, this is a chance to find out that Jesus is a friend.

JONATHAN AND DAVID

David was a shepherd when he helped the Israelite army to beat the Philistines by killing Goliath. Saul, the Israelite king, was delighted with David's victory and took him to live in his palace. David became great friends with Saul's son Jonathan. They made a pact to be friends forever. Jonathan sealed the pact by giving David his clothes, his sword, and bow and arrows.

Jonathan and David became great friends

JESUS

In Jesus we can see that true friendship is a two-way bond. Jesus loved and helped his friends; he also wanted their friendship. These are examples.

• Sharing knowledge: Jesus said, 'I've called you friends, for everything that I learned from my father I've made known to you.'

• Loyalty: Jesus stuck by his friends, even when they let him down. After Jesus' arrest, Peter denied knowing him three times. When Jesus was brought back to life after being crucified, he went to find Peter and forgave him.

• Support: Just before he was arrested, Jesus asked his friends to be with him and pray with him.

Jesus prays with his friends

• Protection: When the soldiers arrested Jesus, he said, 'I'm the one you want. Let these men go.' The disciples were allowed to go.

• Love: Jesus said, 'Greater love has no one than this, that he lay down his life for his friends.' And that's what Jesus did.

Bible Search

• A friend loves:
Proverbs 17:17

• Jesus: *John 15:12–15*

• A friendship meal:
Revelation 3:20

• Jonathan and David:
1 Samuel 18:1–4; 20:1–42; 23:16–18

A medium

GHOSTS
AND DEMONS

There is a great deal of interest today in the occult. Occult means supernatural, mystical, perhaps evil, forces which are beyond our understanding. The Bible speaks very strongly on this subject. It says: 'Let no one be found among you who…is a medium or spiritist or who consults the dead. Anyone who does these things is detestable to the Lord.'

GHOSTS

Many people tell weird stories about ghosts. Ghosts are supposed to be the spirits of dead people who haunt the Earth. There's no hint at all in the Bible that dead people come back to this world. (See the page on Heaven.)

A ghost

Demons may control people

DEMONS

In the Gospel stories, demons (evil spirits) are very active, causing illness and madness, and controlling people. The stories show that Jesus came to the world to destroy the power of evil.

EXORCISM

Exorcism means driving away demons, ghosts or spirits with the power of Jesus. Special religious services and blessings are carried out to do this.

STEER CLEAR

God protects people from demons. But people who go out of their way to get in touch with evil spirits risk being taken over by them. This is one reason why the Bible forbids seances (meetings where people attempt to receive messages from the spirits of the dead).

Isaiah wrote: 'When men tell you to consult mediums and spiritists, who whisper and mutter, should not a people enquire of their God? Why consult the dead on behalf of the living?'

Paul said, 'Whatever is true, whatever is noble, whatever is right, whatever is pure, whatever is lovely… think about such things.' And Jesus said, 'I am the way, the truth and the life.'

Paul told people to think of what is pure and lovely

See also the page on Superstition and Magic.

Bible Search

- Detestable things: **Deuteronomy 18:9–13**
- Wise words: **Philippians 4:8**
- A waste of time: **Isaiah 8:19**
- Jesus: **Matthew 12:22–29; John 14:6**

GIVING AND TAKING

Life is a gift given to us by God. And God 'richly provides us with everything for our enjoyment'. But his best gift was Jesus. John wrote: 'God so loved the world that he gave his only Son, that whoever believes in him should not perish but have everlasting life.'

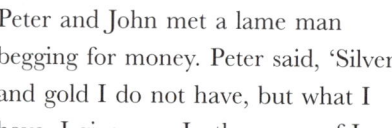

Peter and John help a lame man

GREED

Humans are greedy. We want to take the best things for ourselves, or we take more than we need. We are greedy for all kinds of things: food, money, power, medals, fame, toys, and information. Our greed can get us into a lot of trouble.

Greedy for food

ZACCHAEUS

Zacchaeus was a tax-collector. He was a bad man who cheated and robbed the taxpayers. But then he met Jesus, and he changed. He gave half his things away, and he paid back four times the money he had stolen.

A LAME MAN

Peter and John met a lame man begging for money. Peter said, 'Silver and gold I do not have, but what I have, I give you. In the name of Jesus Christ of Nazareth, walk.' We too should help people when we can.

THE GOOD GIVING GUIDE

In Paul's letter to the Corinthians, he said that people should give cheerfully and generously. In Matthew, Jesus told people not to make a big thing of giving, just so that other people would admire them. He told them that they should give generously, but keep quiet about it instead.

For more about giving, turn to the pages on Money and People in Need.

ADAM AND EVE

Adam and Eve, the first man and woman, were greedy for the fruit which God had forbidden them to eat, because the Devil had promised it would give them power. When they disobeyed God and ate the fruit, their action was the start of all the trouble in the world.

Bible Search

- A cheerful giver:
  2 Corinthians 9:7–11
- God's gifts:
  1 Timothy 6:17; John 3:16
- A lame man:
  Acts 3:1–10

28

GOD WHO IS HE?

In the Old Testament, names were important. A person's name described what he or she was like. God called his son 'Jesus', because the word meant 'the Lord saves'.

It is impossible for one word to sum up everything about God. But some of the names used to describe God tell us a little about him.

David and Goliath

YAHWEH

'Yahweh' is often translated as 'Lord' in our Bibles. It used to be translated as 'Jehovah', but that was incorrect.

One day, Moses was looking after sheep in the mountain land called Midian. Suddenly, he saw a bush on fire. He went closer, and there God told him to rescue the Israelites from Egypt. 'Who are you?' asked Moses. God replied, 'YHWH'. The Hebrew language had no vowels, and these are consonants. The word probably means 'the God who is always present'.

ABBA

Abba

The Jews had always known that God was their father. But Jesus showed them the full meaning of the word. He called God 'Abba', a word meaning 'Daddy'.

God is the strong, loving father who is an example to all parents.

Through faith in Jesus, we are all God's children.

JUDGE

God judges and punishes wrong. In the end, no one gets away with evil. Jesus will come at the end of the world to judge evil. God forgives those who trust Jesus.

GOD OF ARMIES

David walked out by himself towards the great giant, Goliath. 'I'll make mincemeat of you,' sneered Goliath. 'You have your sword, spear and javelin,' David said. 'But I come to you in the name (the power) of the God of armies…'

The name 'God of armies' shows that God is all-powerful and fights for his people. Today, our battles are against lack of love and trust in God.

Moses and the burning bush

Bible Search

- God of armies: **I Samuel 17:15**
- Judge: **Genesis 18:25**
- Yahweh: **Exodus 3:1–14**
- Today's battles: **Ephesians 6:10–20**

GOD AND HIS ACTIONS

Who is God? What is he like? In the Bible, we see that God controlled the events which are described. God made our planet and everything in it. From this we see his incredible power. By looking at what someone does, we can tell what sort of person they are. Here are some of the things we know about God from his actions.

THE ISRAELITES' ESCAPE

When the Jews wanted to describe God, they looked back to when he led them out of Egypt in the Exodus. Here we see:

- God's love. He saved people who were weak and miserable, because he loved them.
- God's power. God sent plagues to Egypt. He led the slaves to freedom through the sea. In miracle after miracle, he gave them water and food. Nothing was too hard for God.

The parting of the sea

- God's goodness. On Mount Sinai, God gave the people his laws. He wanted his people to keep his laws, and live good lives.

- God's holiness. God came to Mount Sinai in darkness, storm and lightning. The whole mountain smoked and quaked. But the people never saw God. He doesn't have a physical body.

Mount Sinai

Bible Search

- God's love and power: **Psalm 136**
- God on Mount Sinai: **Deuteronomy 4:15–16; Hebrews 12:18–20**
- God's love: **John 3:16**
- The cross: **1 Peter 2:24**

THE EXILE AND RETURN

God wanted his people to love and trust him. When the people worshipped other gods, King Nebuchadnezzar destroyed the Temple and took the people as prisoners to Babylonia. God used King Nebuchadnezzar as his agent to teach the people a lesson.

King Nebuchadnezzar destroys the Temple

JESUS

In Jesus, we see God's forgiving love in action, in a human life. John wrote: 'God so loved the world that he gave his one and only son, that whoever believes in him shall not perish but have everlasting life.'

Jesus

(Turn also to the page headed Trinity.)

30

GOD LOOKING FOR

The fool says there is no God

God is beyond our understanding. If we knew everything about God, he would no longer be God. The Bible never sets out to 'prove' God exists, but takes it for granted. The opening words of Genesis are: 'In the beginning… God…'

A psalmist said that atheists (people who don't believe in God) are fools: 'The fool says in his heart, "There is no God."'

DON'T KNOWS

Some people take pride in saying they're not sure if God exists. The Bible's answer to these people (agnostics) is: 'You will seek me and find me when you seek me with all your heart. I will be found by you.'

Instead of saying, 'I'm not sure if God exists,' agnostics should ask themselves, 'Do I want to find God?'

Agnostics should ask themselves 'Do I want to find God?'

Bible Search

- Finding God: *Jeremiah 29:13*
- Thomas: *John 20:24–29*
- Taste and see: *Psalm 34:8*
- Jesus' story of the lost sheep: *Luke 15:1–7*

GOD SEEKS US

There is a big difference between the Christian faith and all other religions. Christianity teaches that God came to find us. Jesus said, 'I have come to seek and search for the lost.'
The prophet Ezekiel said God was like a shepherd looking for his lost sheep. He would 'search for the lost and bring back the strays… bind up the injured and strengthen the weak.'

DOUBTING THOMAS

When Thomas saw Jesus after the resurrection, Jesus said, 'Look at my hands… stop doubting and believe…Because you have seen me, you believe; blessed (happy) are those who have not seen me and yet believe.'

TASTE AND SEE

In the end, we cannot prove or disprove the existence of God. The first step to knowing God is a step of faith. This means believing in him, praying to him and obeying Jesus, without proof he exists. Christian teaching is that as time goes on, we will come to know God for ourselves, from our own experience. This is what the psalmist means when he says, 'Taste and see that the Lord is good.'

GOSSIP
AND FINDING FAULT

Gossiping

It sometimes seems as though everybody talks behind other people's backs, and enjoys nasty gossip. Jesus had some tough words to say about gossip: 'People will have to explain every careless thing they have said. This will happen on the Day of Judgment.'

Bible Search

- Judged by what you say: **Matthew 12:36–37**
- Gossip: **Proverbs 10:8; 18:8; 26:20**
- Plank versus speck: **Matthew 7:1–5**

GOSSIP

The writer of The Book of Proverbs had wise words on gossip:
- 'The words of a gossip are like tasty bits of food. People take them all in.'
- 'Foolish talk will lead to your ruin.' (People don't trust a gossip.)
- 'Without wood, a fire will go out. Without gossip, quarrelling will stop.'

People take in gossip like crows pecking for tasty morsels

FINDING FAULT

We find it all too easy to find fault with other people. We might describe them as stupid or weedy. But Jesus warned: 'Don't judge other people, and you will not be judged. You will be judged in the same way that you judge others.'

Sometimes we decide that someone else has acted wrongly. But we do not have to make nasty remarks about them because of it.

PLANK VERSUS SPECK

A carpenter

Jesus told people not to be hypocrites. He said, 'Why do you look at the speck of sawdust in your brother's eye and pay no attention to the plank (of wood) in your own eye? How can you say to your brother, "Let me take the speck out of your eye," when all the time there is a plank in your own eye?'

Finding fault

In the busy markets of Jesus' day, carpenters were often seen carrying long planks of wood over their shoulders. Everyone would have known what Jesus meant by having a plank of wood in your eye!

HOPE

Paul said, 'When you talk, do not say harmful things. But say what people need: words that will help others become stronger.'

Jesus said that the Holy Spirit would help Christians know the right words to say.

Say things to help others

32

Showing kindness

GRACE GOD'S LOVE

God is love. This idea is the basis of all Christian belief. God's love is active and powerful. Grace means God's loving kindness to people who do not deserve it.

The word 'grace' is not used in the Old Testament, but the idea is there. Words like 'mercy' and 'kindness' reflect it.

JESUS

The New Testament writers took the Greek word for grace, and gave it a new meaning. It stood for the love God showed when he sent Jesus to die on the cross. Paul wrote: 'By grace you are saved through faith.'

Showing love

Saying grace before a meal

SAYING GRACE

Grace is also the short prayer we say to give thanks or ask for blessing. The words 'The grace of the Lord Jesus be with you' mean 'May you go on knowing Jesus' love, care and forgiveness.'

Bible Search

- Saved by grace: *Ephesians 2:8*
- Throne of grace: *Hebrews 4:16*
- Jesus: *John 1:16–17*
- Grace for a problem: *2 Corinthians 12:9*

GRACE TO BE STRONG

Paul had a problem. He prayed, but it didn't go away. But he was able to live with it because God gave him grace. 'My grace is all you need,' God said.

This gift of God's love and strength is given to people who know they need Jesus.

Paul prays for help

THE THRONE OF GRACE

The writer of Hebrews calls God's throne a 'throne of grace'. By 'throne' he meant the central point of God's power. 'Let us approach the throne of grace with confidence,' the writer says, 'so that we may…find grace to help us in our time of need.' He meant God listens to our prayers and answers them.

33

GREEN ISSUES

The Earth is in crisis. From the television and newspapers, we hear terrible stories of the destruction of our planet. But there is also good news. Many hundreds of thousands of people all over the world are taking part in the the battle to save the Earth.

Rainforest

A FEW FACTS

- Rainforests: If present trends continue, the world's rainforests will be destroyed within fifty years.
- A layer of gas called the ozone layer, shields the Earth from the sun's harmful rays. But now it has a hole in it which is the size of the USA.
- Half of West Germany's trees are dying because of acid rain.
- Nuclear waste has polluted the seas. Plutonium from nuclear reactors remains lethal after 240,000 years.

This list could go on and on.

GOD'S EARTH

'The Earth is the Lord's,' said a psalm writer. God wants us to look after the Earth and bring the best out of it.

We should not use up all the Earth's resources. When God gave the people manna to eat in the desert, he told them not to take more than they needed. People who were greedy and took too much found that it went rotten.

Jewish teachers taught that leftover food should be kept and not thrown away. When Jesus fed 5,000 people, he told his friends to collect all the leftover food. Jesus said, 'Watch out and guard yourselves against every form of greed.'

WHAT CAN WE DO?

The best ways for us to help look after the Earth are to:
- Educate ourselves, and find 'green' ways of living.
- Stand up against pollution and the wrong use of resources. Boycott the products of bad companies.
- Pray and support people who are working to save planet Earth.

Finding out how to look after the Earth

Bible Search

- God's world: **Psalm 8:6; 24:1–2**
- Greed: **Luke 12:15; 1 Timothy 6:10**
- Manna: **Exodus 16:14–20**

GUIDANCE
BY DREAMS AND SIGNS

We see how God loves and guides his people over and over again in the Bible. It's rather like a theme tune that is repeated during a film.

God's guidance was sometimes simple and clear. When the Israelite slaves escaped from Egypt and went into the desert, they were often led by a pillar of cloud during the day, and a pillar of fire at night.

Bible Search

- God guides: *Isaiah 63:14*
- Gideon: *Judges 6:36–40*
- A warning: *Deuteronomy 13:1–5; Matthew 12:38–39*

GIDEON

God told Gideon to fight the enemy invaders. Gideon was scared, and asked God for a sign that Israel would be saved. He put sheep's wool on the ground and prayed for it to be first wet, when the ground was dry, and then dry when the ground was wet. God did as he asked.

Gideon puts sheep's wool on the ground

DREAMS

God spoke to his people through dreams in times of particular danger and change, for example when Joseph was taken to Egypt and sold as a slave; when the Israelites were captured and taken off into exile; and when Jesus was born.

COWS

An Egyptian pharaoh dreamt that seven fat cows came out of the Nile. Seven thin, ugly cows followed them and ate up the fat cows. Nobody could tell him what his dreams meant until Joseph, who had been kept in prison, was brought before him. Joseph told the pharaoh that the dream meant there was going to be a famine. The pharaoh was impressed and made Joseph his chief minister. Joseph was able to save the people from starvation, by storing up lots of grain before famine struck.

Joseph orders grain to be stored

Dreams

OUR DREAMS

Most of our dreams have no special meaning. But sometimes a powerful dream can help us, not because it's a message for other people, but because it tells us about ourselves. A bad dream may show us that we're scared or worried, and may need to talk to someone about a problem.

35

GUIDANCE
MAKING DECISIONS

In Old Testament times, God guided his people by dreams, voices, signs, visions, and prophecies. God used some of these methods in New Testament times, and still does today. But the chief way he guides us is by the example of Jesus, and by giving us the Holy Spirit. A psalmist said, 'He guides the humble in what is right and teaches them his way.'

Understanding from those who love us

THE HOLY SPIRIT

Jesus said to his friends, 'The Holy Spirit will guide you into all truth.' Sometimes people talk of the Holy Spirit 'speaking' to them. They don't mean they hear a human voice. They mean an idea has come into their mind, or everything has clicked into place. They know that this has come from God, partly because they now feel very peaceful. Paul said, 'And the peace of God…will guard your hearts.'

Everything clicks into place

THE BOOK OF ACTS

In Acts we see how the Holy Spirit guides Christians:
- *By prayer.*
When the Christians in Antioch were praying, the Holy Spirit told them to send out missionaries. Prayer doesn't always change things around us, but it can change the way we think and feel.

Praying

- *By the life and words of Jesus.*
Jewish leaders told Jesus' friends to stop preaching, but they said, 'We must obey God rather than men.' We can test our 'guidance' by making sure it agrees with the teaching of Jesus, and the Bible.

Reading the Bible

- *Through people.*
God sometimes gives extra gifts of understanding to people in the Church or to people who love us. These people can often help us.

Understanding from people in the Church

- *Through circumstances.*
God is in control of events. We can often tell what he wants by what happens.
For example, the early Christians had to decide whether to let non-Jews be part of the Church. After a lot of discussion, they finally decided that they would, when Paul told them what God was doing, and Peter told them what the Bible said.

Bible Search

- A big problem: **Acts 15**
- A promise: **Psalm 25:9**
- Putting God first: **Acts 5:29**
- Peace: **Philippians 4:7**
- Truth: **John 16:13**

ANY QUESTIONS
1. Why did the apostles disobey the Jewish leaders?
2. How do we know if the guidance other people give us is good?

HAPPINESS THROUGH CHRISTIAN FAITH

The Christian faith is not gloomy. When Jesus was born, the angel said, 'I bring you good news of great joy.' And not long before he died, Jesus said to his friends, 'I have told you this so that my joy may be in you, and your joy may be complete.'

THE SERMON ON THE MOUNT

One day, Jesus and his friends went up a mountain. He sat down and started to talk about how he wanted his friends to live in the world. Jesus began with a poem that we call 'the Beatitudes'.

Jesus recites the Beatitudes

Bible Search

- Beatitudes: *Matthew 5:1–10*
- Angels' news: *Luke 2:10*
- The joy of Jesus: *John 15:11*

THE BEATITUDES

The word comes from a Latin word meaning 'happy'. Many people reading the Beatitudes might say, 'That's not my idea of happiness!' But the poem describes an inner happiness that God gives as his gift to people who live in his way.

Beatitude
Meaning

Blessed are the poor in spirit
People who can't cope without God.

Blessed are those who mourn
People who feel very sad about the wrong things in themselves and in the world.

Blessed are the meek
Those who give way to other people.

Blessed are those who hunger
People who long for right things to be done and thirst for righteousness.

Blessed are the merciful
People who are kind.

Blessed are the pure in heart
Those who are sincere when they pray, and help other people.

Blessed are the peacemakers
People who work to get rid of bitterness, anger and wrong.

Blessed are those who are persecuted because of righteousness
People are are laughed at and treated badly because they are loyal to Jesus.

HEALING AND HEALTH

King Asa

In Old Testament times, health was seen as a sign of God's blessing. The Israelites believed firmly that as God had created them, so he could cure their illnesses. The Old Testament criticized one king, Asa, because he had a bad foot disease and 'did not seek help from the Lord, but only from doctors'.

HEALTH AND WHOLENESS

To the Israelites, health meant being well in body, in spirit, and in mind. They had a proverb about this: 'Being cheerful keeps you healthy. It is slow death to be gloomy all the time.'

Being cheerful

Being gloomy

JESUS

Wherever Jesus went, he healed people who were ill. These healings were a sign that God had come to the Earth. As well as healing people's bodies, Jesus also healed their spirits, by forgiving their sins. This is what he meant when he said, 'My peace I give you.'

THE EARLY CHURCH

When Paul sailed to Rome, he was shipwrecked on the island of Malta. While he was there, he met a man in bed with a fever. Paul prayed, laid his hands on the man, and healed him. After that, other people on the island came to Paul to be healed. Paul later wrote that the Holy Spirit gave some Christians the gift of healing.

James wrote that when Christians were ill, they should ask their church leaders to pray for them to be healed.

Bible Search

- King Asa: *2 Chronicles 16:12*
- Being cheerful: *Proverbs 17:22*
- Forgiving sins: *Mark 2:1–12*
- On Malta: *Acts 28:7–9*
- God's power: *2 Corinthians 12:7–10*
- Healing gifts: *1 Corinthians 12:28*

STILL ILL?

God's healing often comes through doctors (one of the early disciples, Luke, was a doctor). But disease affects everyone, because it is part of an imperfect world. People who follow God can still suffer. Paul had an illness that would not go away. God promised to be with Paul and to give him strength to work for God despite his illness. Paul's illness made him rely more on God; it was not a punishment for his sins or lack of faith.

Paul had an illness that would not go away

ANY QUESTIONS

1 Why do you think God gave some of the early Christians the power to heal?
2 How would Paul's illness have made him rely more on God?

HEAVEN
AND HELL

The word 'heaven' has two meanings in the Bible. Firstly, it means everything that God has created beyond the Earth. Secondly, it means God's home, where God rules as king, and his wishes are always obeyed.

Just before he was killed, Jesus said to his friends, 'Trust in God. Trust also in me. In my Father's house are many rooms. If it were not so, I would have told you. I am going there to prepare a place for you.'

John described heaven as a sea of glass

IS HEAVEN A PLACE?

Heaven may not be an actual place, as we understand it. It's not another planet, for example. It's easier to think of heaven as another dimension. John said, 'Everyone who believes in him will have eternal life.' This is God's life of love and happiness, outside time.

It is easier to think of heaven as another dimension

A PICTURE

In the Book of Revelation, John tried to describe heaven. He talked about music, singing, light, a great sea of glass, and flashing lightning. God's throne looked as if it was made of shining jewels and a rainbow.

In heaven, John saw crowds of people praising God. He wrote: 'Never again will they hunger. Never again will they thirst. ...And God will wipe away every tear from their eyes.'

HELL

The Greek word 'gehenna' is often translated as 'hell'. Gehenna was a rubbish dump outside Jerusalem, where a fire was kept burning to destroy the rubbish.

Jesus talked of 'the darkness'. Hell is being cut off from God. Some people think hell goes on forever. Others say that those who don't go to heaven are wiped out forever.

WHO GOES TO HEAVEN?

Those people who trust Jesus to forgive them, and who obey him by living in loving ways, can go to heaven. John wrote: 'Whoever believes in him shall not perish but have eternal life.'

See also the pages on End of the World, and Ghosts.

Gehenna, the rubbish dump outside Jerusalem

Bible Search

- Many rooms: **John 14:1–4**
- A throne in heaven: **Revelation 4**
- A song in heaven: **Revelation 7:15–17**
- Hell: **Matthew 8:12; 25:41–46**

HOLINESS

Think of a blazing fire, white-hot in the centre, so bright that you can't look at it. The prophet Ezekiel said God looked like glowing metal with fire inside it. And from his waist down he looked like fire. We know that God is not really a fire. The prophet Ezekiel used the description to help us understand the holiness of God.

Bible Search

- A holy person: *Colossians 3:12–14*
- God as a fire: *Ezekiel 1:27; Hebrews 12:29*
- In training: *1 Corinthians 9:24–27*
- God's command: *1 Peter 1:13–16*

A HOLY GOD

When we say God is holy, we mean:
- He is completely good. One day, he will get rid of everything that is bad.
- He is utterly different from us. God's holiness is the goodness and greatness which shines out of him. It is seen best in Jesus.

A BURNING BUSH

Moses

One day, Moses saw a bush on fire. A voice said, 'Take off your sandals. You are standing on holy ground.' God was in that bush, so the ordinary ground became holy.

In ways like this, God taught his people that any object he used, shared his holiness. So the word 'holy' came to be applied to anything 'set apart' for God.

A HOLY PEOPLE

In the Old Testament, God gave his people a command: 'Be holy, because I, the Lord your God, am holy.'

In the New Testament, Jesus showed that God's holy people were the people who followed him and obeyed him.

ANY QUESTIONS
1. Why did God tell Moses to take off his sandals?
2. How does a person become holy?

Think of holiness as a blazing fire

THE GIFT OF HOLINESS

We can't make ourselves holy. Holiness is a gift from God. First, God forgives us when we trust Jesus (this is called justification). Then he gives us his Holy Spirit, who helps us to become more and more like Jesus as we obey him (this is called sanctification).

IN TRAINING

Paul said that followers of Jesus were in training, and must not give in to wrong feelings and actions. 'Without holiness no one will see the Lord,' said the writer of the Letter to the Hebrews.

HOLY SPIRIT
WHO IS HE?

The Holy Spirit is God at work in our world. We cannot see him, just as we cannot see the wind. But we can see what the Holy Spirit does, just as we can see what the wind does. The Holy Spirit is not an 'it', but a person. He is what we call God as we experience him in daily life.

The Bible uses symbols, or pictures in words, to describe the Holy Spirit.

Bible Search
- Water: **John 4:14**
- Wind: **John 3:8, Acts 2:2**
- Fire: **Acts 2:3**
- A dove: **John 1:32**

We cannot see the Holy Spirit

WIND, FIRE AND WATER

Old and New Testament words for 'spirit' mean 'spirit', 'wind', or 'breath'. Jesus said the Spirit is like the wind which you cannot see or control. On the Day of Pentecost (see the next page) the Spirit was actually felt like a rushing wind, and seen as fire. In a hot, dry land the most marvellous sight is a leaping spring of fresh, bubbling water. Jesus said the Holy Spirit is like that spring.

DOVE

When Jesus was baptized, the Holy Spirit came to him in the shape of a dove. The dove is a gentle, loving bird, keeping one mate for life.

THE GO-BETWEEN GOD

Jesus said that the Holy Spirit was truth, and Paul wrote that the Holy Spirit gave fellowship. The Holy Spirit helps us to understand and appreciate the world around us. Above all, he points us to Jesus.

The Holy Spirit gives fellowship

THE COUNSELLOR

Jesus called the Spirit a counsellor. A counsellor helped people in trouble with the law. The Holy Spirit helps us in our troubles.

A counsellor

ANY QUESTIONS
1. How did Jesus describe the Holy Spirit?
2. How do we see the Holy Spirit at work in the world?

A dove

41

HOLY SPIRIT
IN THE BIBLE

The Holy Spirit made Samson very strong

We cannot see the Holy Spirit, he is invisible like the wind. But in the Bible we can read about some of the things he has done. The Holy Spirit first appears in the first chapter of Genesis.

GOD'S TASK FORCE

In the Old Testament, the Holy Spirit gave certain men and women the skill to carry out special jobs for God. To Bezalel he gave artistic skills to make God's worship tent, the Tabernacle. Saul was filled with great happiness, in order to praise God. Samson was made extremely strong, so he could fight the enemy. Ezekiel was sent visions and the power to tell people God's word.

The Tabernacle

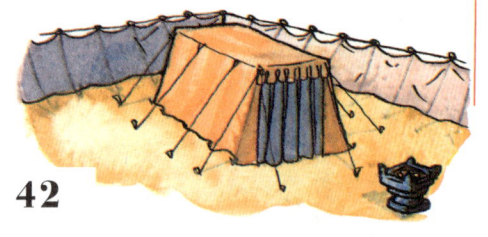

A dove

JESUS

We see the Holy Spirit at work most clearly in the life of Jesus. For example, Jesus did not have a human father. The Holy Spirit made him grow in Mary's womb. When Jesus was baptized, the Holy Spirit appeared in the form of a dove. The Holy Spirit led Jesus into the wilderness, where he was tempted by the Devil. The Holy Spirit gave Jesus the power to free people from evil. With God the Father, the Holy Spirit raised Jesus from the dead.

Bible Search

- Bezalel: *Exodus 31:3*
- Jesus works with the Spirit: *Matthew 12:25–32*
- A promise comes true: *Acts 2:14–21*
- Directing the first Christians: *Acts 13:2–4*

A PROMISE COMES TRUE

In the Old Testament, the Holy Spirit only came to a few people. When Jesus went back to heaven, the Holy Spirit came to everyone who trusted Jesus. This is what God had said would happen.

The Spirit guided the men who wrote the Bible so that they put down the things God wanted us to know.

THE FIRST CHRISTIANS

The Christian church really began fifty days after the death of Jesus, on the day of the Jewish festival of Pentecost. On that day, Jesus sent the Holy Spirit to each of his followers. They were no longer sad and frightened, and began to speak out about Jesus.

The good news of Jesus spread like wildfire. The early Christians acted on the Holy Spirit's orders.

The good news of Jesus spread

HOLY SPIRIT AT WORK TODAY

The Holy Spirit carries out God's plans. He is at work today in the lives of Christians: in the Church, in the world, and in the universe.

He is working to bring about God's rule of peace and love. The prophet Isaiah said that one day the whole world would be full of the knowledge of God, and that would be the work of the Holy Spirit.

JESUS AT THE WELL

One hot afternoon, when Jesus was resting by a well, he said, 'Whoever drinks the water I give him will never thirst...it will become in him a spring of water.' He meant that the Holy Spirit is the gift of Jesus to everyone who obeys him.

NEW BIRTH

When we trust Jesus, we become God's children. This 'second birth' is the work of God's Spirit. In the New Testament, the Spirit is called 'Holy' ninety times. The Spirit makes people holy; that is, like Jesus.

THE GIFTS OF THE SPIRIT

The Spirit gives gifts and skills to Christians. He helps us to pray and understand the Bible. He helps us to be brave and to know what to do. And he helps us to love one another.

Jesus said, 'I am the vine...if you remain in me you will bear much fruit.'

Paul wrote that the 'fruit' of the Spirit was love, joy, peace, patience, kindness, goodness, faithfulness, gentleness and self-control.

ANY QUESTIONS
1 What does the Holy Spirit give to Christians?
2 How do we become God's children?

Jesus said, 'I am the vine...'

The Holy Spirit will guide us

Bible Search
- Future harmony: *Isaiah 11:6–9*
- Jesus at the well: *John 3:4–15*
- The vine and fruit: *John 15:1–8; Galatians 5:22–23*

The Holy Spirit helps us to be brave

HOPE AND ENDURANCE

People today often think there is no hope

The world today is short on hope. Often, people look at the wars, pollution and destruction, and think that there is no hope for the future. When we do speak of hope, the word is often used in a weak sense, for example, 'I hope everything will be all right'. But this is the exact opposite of what the Bible teaches about hope.

HOPE IS...

Christian hope is something definite. It means knowing for certain that in the end, everything is going to be all right. This is because Christian hope is based on the love and goodness of God.

Everything will be all right

HOPE FOR WHAT?

In the New Testament, 'hope' refers to our future in heaven: our own happiness when we see Jesus, and the love and goodness God will give us. It also refers to the time when Jesus will come again.

SO WHAT?

When you are young it is difficult to think of the future

When we are young, the future in heaven often seems far away and unimportant. But God has given those who trust Jesus a sort of deposit, which guarantees future happiness. This deposit is the Spirit of Jesus in us.

Paul called it 'Christ in you, the hope of glory'. Good things will happen, and bad things are nothing to be afraid of.

Bible Search

- Our future hope:
  Ephesians 1:18; 1 John 3:2–3
- Courage from hope:
  2 Corinthians 3:12
- Faith and love from hope:
  Colossians 1:5
- Endurance from hope:
  1 Thessalonians 1:3; Hebrews 10:23–25

A RACE

In a long-distance race, what keeps the runners going for lap after lap? It's the thought of the glory of winning! The writer of the Letter to the Hebrews said that Christian life was like a long-distance race. In this race, everyone who finished would be a winner!

One of the most important teachings in the Bible is that we must persevere, that is to say we must keep going to the end. Hope keeps us going: Paul said, 'We remember your endurance inspired by hope.'

Christian life is like a race

JESUS
WHY HE CAME

Jesus did many things in his life. He showed us what God is really like; he told us how God wants us to live; he gave us an example of a perfect human life. But these weren't the reasons why he came. Jesus told us that he had come in order to die.

Jesus

JESUS' WORDS

Jesus' name for himself was 'the son of man'. This meant 'human being'. Jesus took the name from the Old Testament Book of Daniel.

When Zacchaeus, the hated tax-collector, became a friend of Jesus, Jesus said, 'The son of man came to seek and to save the lost.'

Jesus also said, 'The son of man did not come to be served, but to serve and to give his life as a ransom for many.' Jesus gave his life as a ransom to set us free.

Being set free

SIN

What did Jesus set us free from? Sin means going our own way instead of God's way. People who do this fall into evil ways. Jesus' death is the ransom that sets us free from the power of evil, and from its punishment, which is being cut off from God for ever.

A SUFFERING SERVANT

Jesus called himself a servant, who had 'come to serve'. He was quoting from the Old Testament Book of Isaiah. Isaiah wrote: 'See my servant... He was wounded for the wrong things we did... Each of us has gone his own way. But the Lord has put on him the punishment for all the evil we have done.'

? ANY QUESTIONS
1 Why did Jesus come to die for us?
2 Why did Jesus call himself 'the son of man'?

VICTORY

Jesus said, 'The son of man must suffer...and after three days rise again.' And, 'The son of man will sit on his throne in heavenly glory.' Then, said Jesus, all those who trusted him would be with him for ever.

Bible Search

- The lost: *Luke 19:10*
- A ransom: *Matthew 20:28*
- Suffering servant: *Isaiah 53; 1 Peter 2:22–25*
- Son of man: *Daniel 7:13–14*
- Glory: *Matthew 25:31, 34*

A servant

JESUS THE MAN

Jesus was born about the year 6 BC. He grew up in Nazareth, a town in the northern part of Palestine called Galilee. Until he was about thirty, he was a carpenter. Then he became a travelling teacher and healer. Three years later, the Romans crucified him. Three days later he came back to life. Since then, billions of people have called themselves Christians.

Bible Search

- Jesus has a rest by a well: *John 4*
- Jesus shows his love for people others despised: *Mark 2:15-17*
- Jesus heals people: *Matthew 8, 9*

A REAL HUMAN BEING

Jesus was not an angel, an alien or a superman. Jesus was tempted in every way we are tempted. But he was not weak. He never did anything wrong. When Jesus went into the wilderness for forty days, to fast and pray, the Devil tried to tempt him to stop trusting God. But Jesus refused.

The Devil tempts Jesus

Jesus heals a leper

A MAN FOR OTHERS

Jesus had the power to heal, and he spent his time helping people who were suffering and in need. He showed them how to be happy, forgiving and loving because their father God loved them all.

A MAN AGAINST EVIL

Throughout his life, Jesus fought a battle against evil. His weapons were truth, love and prayer.

Many of the religious leaders at the time kept the rules and ceremonies of their faith carefully, but did not have a close personal knowledge of God or a real care for needy people. Jesus made them face up to their failure to love God and other people.

JESUS IS ALIVE

Mary and Jesus

The Gospel writers do not tell identical stories about Jesus' resurrection. But the main part of their stories is the same: the earth-shattering fact that Jesus died on Friday, and was brought back to life again on Sunday. He was then seen by many people.

BURIAL

Joseph of Arimathea, a rich landowner, and Nicodemus, a member of the Sanhedrin, found the courage to ask Pilate for Jesus' body. They rubbed it with sweet-smelling spices, and wrapped it in cloth. Jesus was then taken to a tomb for burial. The tomb was a cave with a garden in front.

Jesus' body is prepared for burial

The Pharisees were afraid Jesus' friends might steal the body. So Pilate gave them permission to seal the tomb, and put Roman guards on duty. A large stone was rolled in front of the cave.

AN EARTHQUAKE

Very early on Sunday morning, there was an earthquake. An angel, in dazzling white clothes, rolled back the stone and sat on it. The guards were petrified! (Later, the chief priests bribed them to say they had fallen asleep.)

JESUS' FRIENDS

Mary Magdalene, James' mother, and Salome went the tomb to put more spices on Jesus' body. To their amazement, they found that the stone had been rolled away and Jesus' body was gone. The angel said to them, 'Jesus is alive. Tell his friends, and Peter.'

An angel opens the tomb

MARY MAGDALENE

The women raced back and told the disciples, who wouldn't believe them! Peter and John ran to the tomb. They went inside and saw Jesus' burial clothes, but not his body.

As Mary stood crying outside the tomb, a man spoke to her. 'Why are you crying?' he asked. Mary thought it was the gardener. 'Sir, if you've taken the body, tell me where you've put it,' she begged. 'Mary!' said the man. And then she saw he was Jesus.

Bible Search

- Guards: *Matthew 27:62; 28:4, 11–15*
- Burial: *John 19:38–42*
- Peter and John: *John 20:3–9*
- Mary Magdalene: *John 20:10–18*

KINGDOM OF GOD

Jesus' first words when he started preaching were: 'The kingdom of God is near.' The kingdom is not a place, but it exists wherever people obey God. Anyone who lives according to God's rules is part of God's kingdom. This is summed up in the Lord's Prayer: 'Your kingdom come, your will be done on Earth as it is in heaven.'

The kingdom of God is not a place

MIRACLES

Matthew wrote: 'Jesus went through all the towns…preaching the good news of the kingdom and healing every disease.' Jesus' miracles of healing were a sign that he was the Messiah, or deliverer, that the people had been waiting for.

A SEED

Jesus said, 'The mustard seed is the smallest seed, but it slowly grows until it's the biggest plant in the garden, and birds nest in it.' The kingdom of God seemed small to the friends of Jesus, but one day it would be known all over the world.

The growth of a mustard seed

TREASURE

A man and his treasure

Jesus said that the kingdom of God was like a man who finds a treasure hidden in a field and sells everything he has to buy that field. He meant that belonging to the kingdom of God is worth everything you've got.

BELONGING

As members of the kingdom of God, Christians can live worry-free lives. God has promised to give them all they need and to turn even bad things into good.

Jesus said, 'Not everyone who says to me, "Lord, Lord", will enter the kingdom of heaven; but only he who does the will of my Father in heaven.' God's will is that everyone should let him control every part of their lives.

Living a worry-free life

Bible Search

- Entry: *Matthew 7:21*
- God's care: *Matthew 6:25–34*
- Bad into good: *Romans 8:28*

KNOWING YOURSELF

Some people think that a human being is made up of a body with a spirit, or soul, living in it. When a person dies, the spirit flies away, like a bird out of a cage. But in the Bible, the word 'soul' and the word 'body' both mean the same thing: the whole person.

Some people think that the spirit flies away

ME

We can think, choose and act for ourselves; we can feel things and know right from wrong; we can make friends and relate to God. All this makes us unique people. But even if we are hurt or handicapped in some way, so that we can't do all these things, God still knows us and cares for us, and we are special to him.

Everybody is special to God

GOD'S IMAGES

When God made people, he said, 'Let us make man in our image, in our likeness.' This doesn't mean God has a physical body. It means God is a person. We can create, think, and love because that's the way God is.

A PURPOSE

Human beings need to know that their lives have a meaning and purpose. God made us to worship and love him, to love and help other people, and to look after the world.

Paul wrote: 'God gives us all things richly to enjoy.' Everything is a gift from God.

A STORY

Jesus told a story about a rich man who was going on a journey. He gave his money to his three servants to keep until he returned. The first two servants doubled their money. The third servant hid the money in the ground!

When the man came back, he was furious with the third servant and took his money back.

This story showed that we must not waste the abilities God gives us.

The three servants

Bible Search

- God's image: **Genesis 1:26**
- Use our gifts: **Matthew 25:14–30**
- Love: **Mark 12:30–31**

49

LEADERS
AND GOVERNMENTS

Any group of people living or working together needs rules. Leaders decide rules and make sure they are kept. Leaders of a country work together in a government.

When Noah and his family came out of the ark, God said, 'Whoever sheds the blood of man, by man shall his blood be shed.' With those words, God put people in charge of keeping law and order: that was the beginning of government.

Teams need leaders

GOOD GOVERNMENT

In the time of the Judges, there was no government. Everybody 'did what was right in his own eyes', and the result was chaos. Every country needs a good government. That's why the New Testament writers told people to pray for the leaders of governments, and to obey them.

Chaos

BAD GOVERNMENT

In Old Testament times, the leaders of Israel and Judah were often very bad people.

The prophets didn't sit back and say nothing: they got involved, and told the leaders where they were going wrong.

Amos stood up in the marketplace at Bethel and said God would punish the leaders. He complained, 'You trample on the poor and force them to give you grain.'

JESUS

Jesus lived in an occupied country, but he didn't try to rebel against Roman government. He paid his taxes, saying, 'Give to Caesar what is Caesar's.' But Jesus did not respect King Herod, who ruled for the Romans, and hung on to power and wealth by any means. He thought Herod was cunning, like a fox, and refused to answer his questions. The religious leaders had added many extra laws to God's laws. These laws made life hard and did not help people to love God or each other. Jesus refused to keep them.

Taxes

King Herod

A cunning fox

PETER AND JOHN

Peter and John were brought before the Sanhedrin (a council of religious leaders in Jerusalem) and told to stop preaching. 'We must obey God rather than men,' they said.

The Sanhedrin

Bible Search

- Obey leaders and pay taxes: **Romans 13:1–7; 1 Peter 2:13–17**
- Pray for leaders: **1 Timothy 2:2**
- Speaking out: **Jeremiah 21:11–22:19**
- Obey God: **Acts 5:27–29**

LORD'S SUPPER
AND HOLY COMMUNION

The Lord's Supper is also called the Holy Communion, Breaking Bread, the Eucharist (which means 'thanksgiving') and, in Roman Catholic churches, the Mass. It was started by Jesus during his last meal with his friends.

THE PASSOVER

Each year, every Jewish family sits down for a special meal of roast lamb, bitter herbs and unleavened bread. This Passover meal celebrates the time when the Israelites in Egypt were spared by God, while in Egyptian families, every first-born son was killed.

- The first Lord's Supper:
Matthew 26:17–30; John 13–17

- As described by Paul:
1 Corinthians 11:17–26

JESUS' LAST SUPPER

Jesus' last meal with his friends was the Passover meal. During the supper, Jesus broke pieces of bread and gave them to his friends. He said, 'This is my body which is given for you.'

He passed round a cup of wine. He said, This is my blood, the blood of the new covenant, which is shed for the forgiveness of sins.' A covenant is an agreement. In the Old Testament, agreements between God and his people were sealed with a blood sacrifice.

Jesus told his friends to keep on meeting together after his death, and to drink wine and eat bread in the same way, in memory of him.

THE HOLY COMMUNION SERVICE

Receiving communion

Today, Christians eat a small piece of bread (or a wafer) and drink a sip of wine as part of the communion service. There have been many arguments about what Jesus' words at the Last Supper mean, but in Protestant churches most people take communion:
- In memory of Jesus' Last Supper and his death for us.
- As a way of saying that they are sorry for the wrong things they have done.
- As a way of saying that they belong to Jesus and to one another; that they are part of the family (or body) of Jesus.
- As a symbol of their need to receive Jesus' power to live for him.

The Last Supper

LOVE

'I love my mom'

'I love fish and chips.' 'I love my mom.' Our English word 'love' has lots of meanings!

In the New Testament, there are four different words for love. These mean close, loving friendship; the love that you have for your family; love between a man and a woman; and the love God has for his people.

'I love fish and chips'

Bible Search

- Love from God: **1 John 4:7–12**
- Jesus' last command: **John 15:9–17**
- The greatest command: **Mark 12:28–31**
- Who is my neighbour?: **Luke 10:25–37**
- A gift: **Galatians 5:22**

TWO COMMANDS

The New Testament word *agape* means the love God has for his people. It is also the love we are told to show to other people. It means wanting the very best for others, and trying to bring that about.

Someone asked Jesus, 'What is the greatest command?' Jesus replied, 'Love (*agape*) the Lord your God with all your heart, and with all your soul, and with all your mind, and with all your strength. The second is this: "Love your neighbour as yourself."'

Love your neighbour

A STORY

The Samaritan takes the Jew to an inn

'Who is my neighbour?' asked someone else. So Jesus told a story. A Samaritan found a Jew lying on a mountain road, where he had been attacked. He bathed his wounds, took him to an inn and paid the innkeeper to look after him. (This was surprising because Jews didn't like Samaritans.)

So the answer to the question was that anyone who needs your help is your neighbour.

LOVE IS...

What is love like? Jesus gave us a guide. He said, 'Love each other in the way that I have loved you.'

Paul described *agape* love in 1 Corinthians 13. Paul said something startling in this chapter. He said that anything we do for Jesus without love, anything at all, is useless.

Paul said something startling

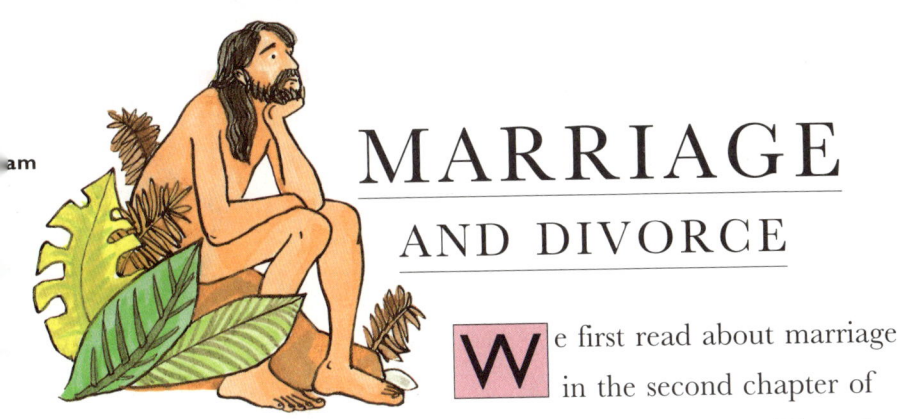

MARRIAGE AND DIVORCE

We first read about marriage in the second chapter of Genesis. Adam was lonely, so God gave him a friend: Eve. Then the writer adds, 'For this reason a man will leave his father and mother and be united to his wife, and they will become one flesh.'

ADULTERY

Commandment number seven in the Ten Commandments is: 'You shall not commit adultery.' This means that husbands and wives must be faithful to each other. They must not have a sexual relationship with another person.

Married people must not be unfaithful

KING DAVID

King David broke the seventh commandment when he fell in love with beautiful Bathsheba, the wife of the soldier Uriah. David made sure Uriah was sent to the front line of the fighting, where he was killed. David then married Bathsheba. God sent Nathan the prophet to tell David how wrong he had been. David was very sorry, and God forgave him.

DIVORCE

In the time of Jesus, a husband was allowed to divorce his wife, but a wife could not divorce her husband. Some Jewish teachers said that a husband could only divorce his wife if she had done something very wrong.

Other teachers said that a husband could divorce his wife for almost any reason: if he didn't like her looks, for example, or if she kept burning the dinner.

A burnt dinner – reason for divorce?

JESUS AND DIVORCE

Jesus was once asked if it was lawful for a man to divorce his wife for any and every reason.

He said that God had never planned that people should divorce at all. The only possible reason for divorce was unfaithfulness.

Paul compared marriage to two oxen

DOUBLE TROUBLE

The Old Testament teachers often said that Jews should not marry people who worshipped other gods. They had different goals in life.

Paul said it was like two oxen, yoked (tied) together to a plough, trying to pull in opposite directions. He advised: 'Do not be yoked with unbelievers… What does a believer have in common with an unbeliever?'

Bible Search

- God's gift: *Genesis 2:24*
- Adultery is wrong: *Exodus 20:14*
- Jesus and divorce: *Matthew 19:1–12*
- Double trouble: *2 Corinthians 6:14–18*

Jesus made lame people able to walk

Jesus cures Jairus' daughter

MIRACLES
IMPOSSIBLE THINGS HAPPEN

A miracle is when God makes something happen that could not happen in any natural way. Jesus made many miracles happen. John's Gospel calls Jesus' miracles 'signs'. They pointed to truths about God.

ASKING FOR A MIRACLE

Sometimes we may pray for a miracle to happen, but it doesn't. God knows better than we do. Sometimes God lets us live with a problem, as a better way of showing his love.

The apostle Paul had a problem: a 'thorn in the flesh'. He prayed for God to work a miracle, but God did not. Instead God said, 'My power is made perfect in weakness.'

Should you ask God to make it stop raining on sports day?

Jesus walks on water

JESUS WALKS ON WATER

Jesus sent his disciples to go ahead of him by boat across the Sea of Galilee. A strong wind blew up, and the disciples found it hard to row. Jesus walked out across the water. When the disciples saw him, they thought Jesus was a ghost and were frightened. Jesus told them not to be afraid, and got into the boat. The wind dropped, and they continued their journey.

JESUS HEALS A LITTLE GIRL

Jairus, who was head of the synagogue, begged Jesus to heal his daughter, who was dying. But by the time they got to Jairus' house, they were told that the girl had died. Jesus said, 'The child is not dead: she is asleep.' He went inside and took hold of the girl's hand, telling her to get up. Immediately, the girl got up and walked about. She was completely better. Everyone was amazed. It was a miracle.

Bible Search

- Jesus on the water: *Mark 6:45–50*
- A storm at sea: *Matthew 8:23–27*
- Paul's thorn in the flesh: *2 Corinthians 12:7–10*
- Jairus' daughter: *Luke 8:40–56*

MONEY A ROOT OF EVIL?

In the Old Testament, people thought that having lots of money was a sign of God's blessing. If you were good, then God loved you and made you rich. That's why Jesus' friends were shocked when he said it was hard for a rich man to get into heaven.

Jesus tells a rich man how to be his follower

A RICH MAN

'I want to belong to your kingdom,' said a rich young man to Jesus. 'What must I do?' 'Keep the Ten Commandments,' said Jesus. 'But I do already,' said the man. 'Give away all your money, and follow me,' said Jesus. The man could not do it.

Jesus told his friends, 'It's hard for a rich person to follow me. It's harder than for a camel to squeeze through the eye of a needle.'

WHAT'S WRONG WITH MONEY?

There's nothing wrong with money: we can use it to do a lot of good. But it's always wrong to rely on money to make us happy.

A TEST

If we spend a lot of time thinking about how to get money, then the love of money has got us in its grip.

Paul said, 'People who want to get rich fall into a trap...Be content with what you have...The love of money is a root of all kinds of evil.'

DON'T WORRY ABOUT MONEY

Jesus said that God fed the birds and he gave the flowers beautiful petals to wear, so he would look after his followers too. By loving God and helping people, followers would get a better sort of wealth: they would gain a happiness that lasted forever.

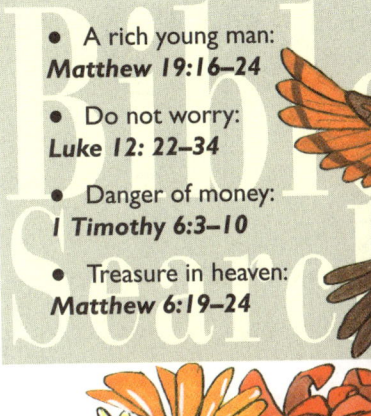

Bible Search
- A rich young man: *Matthew 19:16–24*
- Do not worry: *Luke 12: 22–34*
- Danger of money: *1 Timothy 6:3–10*
- Treasure in heaven: *Matthew 6:19–24*

NAMES
BLASPHEMY, SWEARING

Names are important to us: we like to know their meaning, and we like to give people nicknames. But in Old Testament times, names were even more important. People were careful about naming their babies. They thought that a baby grew to be like his or her name. So, if a stranger told you his name, you thought you knew what sort of person he was.

The name Deborah means 'bee'

THE NAME OF JESUS

Jesus said, 'I am the good shepherd… The good shepherd calls his own sheep.' Jesus meant that he knows us through and through. Jesus said, 'Ask for anything you want in my name and I will do it.' A prayer which asks for something in the name of Jesus must be the sort of prayer that Jesus might make.

THE SONS OF SCEVA

In the town of Ephesus, the seven sons of Sceva claimed to be able to rid people of evil spirits. One day they decided to use Jesus' name to do so. They said to a man with an evil spirit, 'Come out in the name of Jesus.' But the brothers were not Christians and the man attacked all seven of them. This shows Jesus' name is not a magic charm.

The sons of Sceva were attacked

BLASPHEMY

Blasphemy means using God's name in wrong ways. It means telling lies about him to cause trouble, or saying his name aloud because you are in a bad mood. Blasphemy is forbidden in the Ten Commandments. It is hateful for Christians to misuse the name of someone they love.

SWEARING

Swearing means using unpleasant or embarrassing words as a way of getting rid of your angry feelings. It's unkind to upset people by swearing. A lot of today's swearwords were once thought to be blasphemous. But they no longer count as blasphemy because no one remembers their first meaning!

Bible Search

- In the name of Jesus: **John 14:14**
- The sons of Sceva: **Acts 19:11–20**
- The third commandment: **Exodus 20:7**
- The Good Shepherd: **John 10:3**

56

OBEDIENCE
OBEYING GOD

'Love one another'

Jesus said to his friends, 'Not everyone who says to me, "Lord, Lord," will enter the kingdom of heaven, but only he who does the will of my Father which is in heaven.'

Jesus always obeyed God. He said, 'I've come down from heaven not to do my own will, but to do the will of him who sent me.'

TWO BUILDERS

The two houses

Jesus told a story about two men who each set out to build a house. One man built his house on sand; the other built his house on rock. When winter came, rain poured down, hillside steams turned into torrents, and the winds howled. The house on rock remained firm, but the house on sand fell with a great crash.

Jesus said, 'Anyone who hears my words and puts them into practice is like the man who built his house on rock.'

The house on rock survives the storm

JAMES

Jesus' brother, James, said, 'Don't just listen to God's word: do what it says.' James used the example of someone looking into a mirror, seeing a mark on his face, then going away and forgetting to wash it off.

The Bible is like a mirror. It shows us what we need to do, and then we have to do it.

The Bible is like a mirror

Bible Search
- Hard words: **Matthew 7:21**
- Two builders: **Matthew 7:24–27**
- Love: **John 15:17**
- Help: **John 15:5**
- A mirror: **James 1:22–25**

HOW DO WE OBEY GOD?

Jesus was sometimes asked what people need to do to obey God. He gave different answers according to the needs of the person who asked him. One answer was: 'Love one another.'

HELP TO OBEY

As we go about our everyday lives, we sometimes feel we want to do something loving, or to be truthful, or to stand up for Jesus. That idea comes from the Holy Spirit, and Jesus helps us to carry it out.

Do something loving

57

PEACE

Adam and Eve disobeyed God

When God made the world it was filled with peace. This peace was lost when Adam and Eve, the first man and woman, took it into their heads to disobey God. Jesus is often called the Prince of Peace. When he was born, the angels sang: 'Peace on Earth to men with whom God is pleased.'

SHALOM

The Hebrew word for 'peace' is '*shalom*'.

In a person it means wholeness, inner harmony, and knowing you are safe because God is caring for you.

Between people it means trusting and caring; being truthful, forgiving, honest and fair.

In the world, it means taking care of the Earth and the creatures that live there. It means trying to put wrong things, such as pollution, right.

Shalom only comes when people know they are forgiven by God, and when they obey God.

Shalom

THE PRICE OF PEACE

Sin must be punished. That is just and right. Jesus took the punishment we deserve, so that we can be forgiven and be at peace with God. Paul said that Jesus was 'making peace through his blood shed on the cross'.

During his last supper with his friends, Jesus said, 'My peace I give you…'

Bible Search

- Prince of Peace: **Isaiah 9:6**
- Angels' song: **Luke 2:14**
- The price: **Colossians 1:20**
- A gift: **John 14:27**
- Peacemakers: **Matthew 5:9**
- A sword: **Matthew 10:34**

ANY QUESTIONS
1 How did Jesus make us able to be at peace with God?
2 How can Christians be peacemakers?

PEACEMAKERS

Christians should be peacemakers. But this doesn't mean going around with the attitude of 'anything for an easy life'. It means 'making *shalom*'. It may mean giving in to people, and not getting your own way.

In the world, peacemakers often start off by being troublemakers, and challenging things other people do. That's why Jesus once said, 'I did not come to bring peace but a sword.'

Jesus challenges wrong

58

PEOPLE IN NEED
HELPING OTHERS

Many people today are hungry, poor, lonely, ill, or homeless. Many old people feel that nobody cares about them. The Bible writers showed we must do what we can to stop such suffering. Christians used to argue about whether it is more important to trust God to put things right, or to do good ourselves. Today we know that it is essential to do both.

Many old people feel nobody cares about them

STRONG WORDS

Jesus' teaching on helping other people is summed up in a story he told about the end of the world. Then, Jesus said, he would divide Christians into two groups. One group would go with him into heaven. The other group would be sent away.

This is what Jesus said he would say to the first group.

'I was hungry and you gave me food…

I was a foreigner and you took me home with you;

I was in rags and you gave me clothes;

I fell ill and you looked after me…

I was in prison and you came to see me.

When you helped the least of my brothers, you helped me.'

WHAT CAN WE DO?

The poor widow gives money

Sometimes we feel upset because we can't help people very much. But God's idea of help may be different from our own.

Jesus was sitting in the Temple watching people put money in the collection box. Rich people threw in a lot of money. A poor widow gave two tiny coins. Jesus said, 'She put in more than all the others. She put in all she had.'

GIVING

We can give other things besides money, such as our friendship. Zacchaeus was a tax-collector, and people didn't like him. One day he climbed up a tree to see Jesus. He nearly fell down again when Jesus said, 'Zacchaeus, I must stay at your house today.'

Turn also to the page on Giving.

ANY QUESTIONS

1 Jesus taught that Christians must help each other. Why is this so important?
2 How could you help an old person living on their own near you?

Bible Search

- Judgment Day: *Matthew 25:31–46*
- Zacchaeus: *Luke 19:1–27*
- A poor widow: *Luke 21:1–4*

59

PERSECUTION
AND BULLYING

Probably the worst persecution the world has known was by the German Nazis during the Second World War. They murdered over six million Jews in the most horrifying ways.

But persecution takes many other forms. For example, school can be a nightmare place for children who are bullied.

YOU TOO

Many people attack, hurt, kill, and ridicule other people. Jesus said, 'If the world hates you, keep in mind that it hated me first...if they persecuted me, they will persecute you also.' Followers of Jesus don't always fit in with the world's ideas of how to live.

WEAPONS AGAINST PERSECUTION

- Love and prayer.
Stephen was stoned to death for preaching about Jesus, but he prayed for his murderers. Jesus said, 'Love your enemies and pray for those who persecute you.'

- Praise.
The disciples were flogged by the authorities for preaching about Jesus. They came away rejoicing. Peter later wrote: 'If you suffer as a Christian...praise God.'

- Enlist help.
When Paul was a prisoner, his enemies vowed to kill him. Paul's nephew overheard and told Paul, who alerted his guards. As a result he was given an armed escort of 200 soldiers, 70 horsemen and 200 spear-throwers: all to protect one Christian!

- Courage.
Jesus never let fear stop him speaking up. It takes courage to tell teachers about bullying. It's easier to keep quiet. But if people do nothing when they see wrong, the situation gets worse.

It takes courage to tell teachers

- Jesus.
Paul was in court, charged with causing trouble. Everyone deserted him. But he later wrote: 'The Lord stood by my side and gave me strength...The Lord will rescue me from every evil attack.'

School can be a nightmare for children who are bullied

LOVE, NOT REVENGE

The Bible tells us not to seek revenge: it only adds to the hatred and suffering. Instead, Christians are called to love and care for their enemies, and to leave God to deal with people who still go on doing bad things.

Bible Search

- Endure: *1 Corinthians 4:12*
- Rejoice and do good: *1 Peter 4:12–19*
- Holy Spirit's help: *Luke 12:11–12*
- Revenge ruled out: *Romans 12:14, 17–20; Matthew 5:11*

PRAYER THE LORD'S

Jesus talks to his friends

One day, Jesus' friends asked, 'Lord, teach us to pray.' Jesus replied, 'When you pray, say…' and he gave them the prayer we call 'The Lord's Prayer'. The Lord's Prayer is very short. Jesus said, 'When you pray, don't keep babbling on.' He meant that it is better to say a few words and really mean them.

THE LORD'S PRAYER

Our Father
We can trust God to take care of us. He is the father parents ought to copy.

God's example shows us how to be a good parent

In heaven
Heaven, here, means the place where everyone obeys God. It is where the angels are, and where we go when we die. There is more to life than just the world around us.

There is more to life

Hallowed be your name
'Hallowed' means 'holy', and 'name' means 'nature'. God is absolutely good and completely different to us. With these words, we give him our reverence and love.

Your kingdom come, your will be done, On Earth as it is in heaven
'Kingdom' means 'God's rule'. We are praying that we may obey God, and carry out God's plans in the world.

Don't worry about the future

Give us this day our daily bread
'Daily' means 'for the coming day'. It reminds us not to worry about the future, but to pray for the next day. 'Bread' means 'food'. God gives us everything we need.

Forgive us our trespasses As we forgive those who trespass against us
'Trespass' means 'debts' (things we should have done). We are asking God to forgive us, as we must forgive other people.

And lead us not into temptation, but deliver us from evil
'Temptation' means 'tests'. We are asking God to keep us from difficulties that are too hard for us to cope with. The prayer also asks God to keep us safe from the clutches of evil.

Bible Search

- The Lord's Prayer: Matthew 6:9–13; Luke 11:1–4
- The Devil: 1 Peter 5:8

PRAYER QUESTIONS

Prayer is asking God for things such as help and forgiveness. Prayer is talking to God: thanking him, praising him, and telling him how we feel. And prayer also means being silent with God and giving our love to him. 'I look at him and he looks at me,' said one old lady. Sometimes people give rules about prayer, but Jesus never did that.

Bible Search

- Jesus prays:
Mark 1:35; Luke 6:12;
- About everything:
*Philippians 4:6;
1 Thessalonians 5:17*
- Hezekiah's letter:
Isaiah 37:14–20
- With others:
Acts 2:42

WHY PRAY?

Sometimes people ask what point there is in praying, because God knows everything anyway. God is our father. Parents want to hear from their children what they have been doing, even when they already know. They want to talk to their children, and find out what their thoughts are.

Parents like to talk to their children

'I look at him and he looks at me.'

WHERE TO PRAY?

Find a quiet place to pray

Jesus often prayed in quiet places: in a garden, on a hillside, in the country. But he also prayed with his friends. Nehemiah prayed while he built the walls of Jerusalem, which was a very noisy spot. It's not always easy to find a quiet place to pray, but we can make a quiet place in our minds wherever we are.

PAUL IN CORINTH

There are no rules about how long a prayer should be. Sometimes Jesus made quick 'arrow prayers', and sometimes he prayed all night.

We don't have to get on our knees to pray. The best position is one which you find comfortable. People often say, 'Close your eyes and put your hands together.' This is to help you concentrate.

WHAT TO PRAY?

Paul said, 'Do not be anxious about anything, but in everything, by prayer and petition, with thanksgiving, present your requests to God.' We can pray about anything, from the smallest thing to something very important. King Hezekiah prayed about a difficult letter.

WILL I HEAR GOD SPEAKING?

God doesn't use a human voice when he speaks to us. But he speaks by giving us a new idea, or with words in the Bible, or through things that happen.

God does not have a human voice

62

PRAYER PROBLEMS

Praying is one of the most important things Christians can do. That's why people say, 'When Christians pray, the Devil trembles.'

Sometimes, people find it difficult to pray. These are some of the problems they experience.

NOTHING HAPPENS

Often, nothing seems to happen when we pray. But later, we notice changes. Someone said, 'When I stop praying, the coincidences stop happening.'

Sometimes the change is not in the things around us, but in the way we understand them. This happened to David (look at Psalm 73).

Sometimes nothing seems to happen

HOW DOES A PRAYER WORK?

How prayer works is a mystery. But often it's as if God waits for us to pray, so that we can have the happiness of seeing him at work in the world, and of sharing in that work. James said, 'You don't have, because you don't ask God.'

Jesus told a story to encourage people not to give up on prayer. There was once a wicked judge. A poor widow kept coming to him, saying she'd been wronged. The judge took no notice. In the end, he was so fed up with her that he gave her what she wanted. Jesus meant that if a wicked judge could help a widow, how much more God would help his people.

ANSWERING PRAYERS

Sometimes we ask for wrong things in our prayers, so God won't answer them.

Jesus said that prayer asked 'in his name' would be answered. This means prayers that match what Jesus is like. Sometimes Jesus asks us to wait for our prayers to be answered. Once, a message was brought to Jesus to say that his friend Lazarus was ill. Jesus did nothing. Lazarus died. But then, Jesus showed his power by bringing Lazarus to life again.

Jesus learns Lazarus is ill

CONCENTRATING

Some people find that their mind wanders while they are praying. The best thing to do is to try to make these thoughts part of their prayers.

The wicked judge

Bible Search
- A widow: *Luke 18:1–8*
- Prayer in Jesus' name: *John 15:16*
- A loving Father gives good gifts: *Matthew 7:7–11*
- Showing-off prayers get nowhere: *Matthew 6:5–6; Luke 18:9–14; James 4:2–3*

PREJUDICE
FIGHTING AGAINST

Prejudice means disliking someone for no good reason, usually because they are different to you in some way, such as by their sex, race or religion. To know what the Bible teaching is on this, we have only to look at the life of Jesus. He fought against prejudice of every kind.

We are all different to each other in many ways

MONEY

Poor people were often treated as though they were very unimportant. But Jesus didn't think that money made a person important. He chose to be poor.

James wrote: 'Suppose a man comes into your meeting wearing a gold ring and fine clothes, and a poor man in shabby clothes also comes in. Don't treat the rich man better than the poor man. God has chosen the poor in this world to be rich in faith.'

A rich man

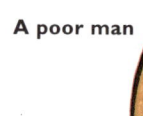

A poor man

FOREIGNERS

The Jews were especially prejudiced against Samaritans. But Jesus told a story in which the hero was a Samaritan.

A Jewish man was travelling to Jericho, when he was attacked by thieves and left by the roadside. A powerful priest came past, but took no notice of the man. Some time later, a Levite came along the road. He too ignored the injured man. Then a Samaritan came by, and went to help the man straight away.

WOMEN

In Bible times, women were treated like servants. They had no rights. Jesus showed this was wrong by his actions. For example, the first person Jesus appeared to, when he was brought back to life, was not Peter or John, but Mary Magdalene.

Jesus had many friends who were women, and he treated them with great kindness. He often spoke to women he didn't know in public: this was against Jewish custom.

Jesus speaks to a woman he doesn't know

BACKGROUND

Jesus grew up in Galilee. People who came from Galilee had a distinctive accent, which was looked down on by people in other parts of the country.

Some of Jesus' friends were uneducated and poor, but he was also friends with powerful and clever people. Jesus was not prejudiced against anyone.

SUMMING UP

Paul wrote: 'For Christians, there is no difference between people of different races. There is no difference between male and female. You are all the same to Jesus.'

Bible Search

- The first witness: *John 20:10–18*
- Rich and poor: *Luke 21:1–4; James 2:2-5*
- A woman in public: *John 4*
- The Good Samaritan: *Luke 10:25–37*

PRIESTS AND PROPHETS

In Old Testament times, people depended on prophets and priests to teach them what God wanted. In the time of Moses, all priests came from the family of Aaron (Moses' brother); later other members of the tribe of Levi also took on priestly duties. The job of High Priest (the leader of the priests) was passed on from father to son.

PRIESTS

The main work of a priest was to explain God's laws; offer sacrifices and pray for the people; look after the Tabernacle and, later, the Temple. Priests were divided into twenty-four groups, which took it in turns to do a week's Temple duty.

The High Priest wore a special breastplate, which had twelve precious stones set in gold.

The High Priest

PROPHETS

Prophets gave advice

Prophets were men and women chosen by God to give the people his messages. They told people how they should live in order to please God.

Some prophets were king's advisers; some went to war (like army chaplains today); some gave guidance about problems. Sometimes prophets lived together in groups.

- The breastplate: **Exodus 28:15–30**
- Zechariah on duty: **Luke 1:5–10**
- Groups of prophets: **1 Samuel 10:10; 2 Kings 4:1**
- Nathan: **2 Samuel 12:1–10**
- A priest's work: **Deuteronomy 33:10**

NATHAN

A poor man and his pet lamb

When King David fell in love with Bathsheba, he had her husband sent into battle where he knew he would be killed.

The prophet Nathan came to see David. Nathan said, 'A poor man had one pet lamb. It ate at his table, and slept in his arms. But a rich man killed it for a party. You are like that man.' David realized how wrong he had been.

AFTER THE EXILE

During the Jews' exile in Babylonia, the work of teaching God's laws was taken over by scribes.

When there was no king, the priests became the leaders of the people. The High Priest was leader of the Sanhedrin (a council of religious leaders in Jerusalem), and the chief priests were members of it.

A scroll for teaching

PROMISES
AND AGREEMENTS

We rely on people to do what they say they will do. If people keep breaking their promises, it causes trouble. For example, when a husband and wife break their marriage promises, the marriage breaks down.

All through the Old Testament, we read how God promises to care for the people he loves, but those same people keep betraying him.

If you promise to play with your sister, then you should do so

NOAH

God often entered into a bond, or pact, with people, called a covenant. After the Flood, God made a covenant with Noah. God promised that he would never again destroy the Earth in such a way, until the end of time. As a sign of this, God made a rainbow.

ABRAHAM

God made a covenant with Abraham. He promised that Abraham would have as many descendants as there were grains of sand on the seashore. Abraham had only to believe God.

MOSES

Through Moses, God made a covenant with the Israelites. God promised to look after the people, if they would keep his laws. If not, trouble would come. The people broke their promise to God, and God kept his promise about the trouble.

The Ten Commandments

Bible Search

- Abraham: **Genesis 15; 22:17**
- A new covenant: **Hebrews 8:7–13**
- Jesus' death makes it possible: **Hebrews 9:15**
- Yes and no: **Matthew 5:37**

A seashore

A NEW COVENANT

The prophet Jeremiah said that one day, God would make a new covenant with his people.

At the Last Supper, Jesus told his friends that he was about to bring in the new covenant. His death would make it possible. Anyone, man, woman and child, could enter into an agreement with Jesus. The agreement would be based on love.

Food at the Last Supper

KEEPING YOUR WORD

Jesus said that people must keep their word. There was no need to swear oaths (our modern version might be to say things like 'cross my heart'). Jesus said people should say a simple 'yes' and 'no' and stick to it.

A Hindu goddess

RELIGIONS
OTHER BELIEFS

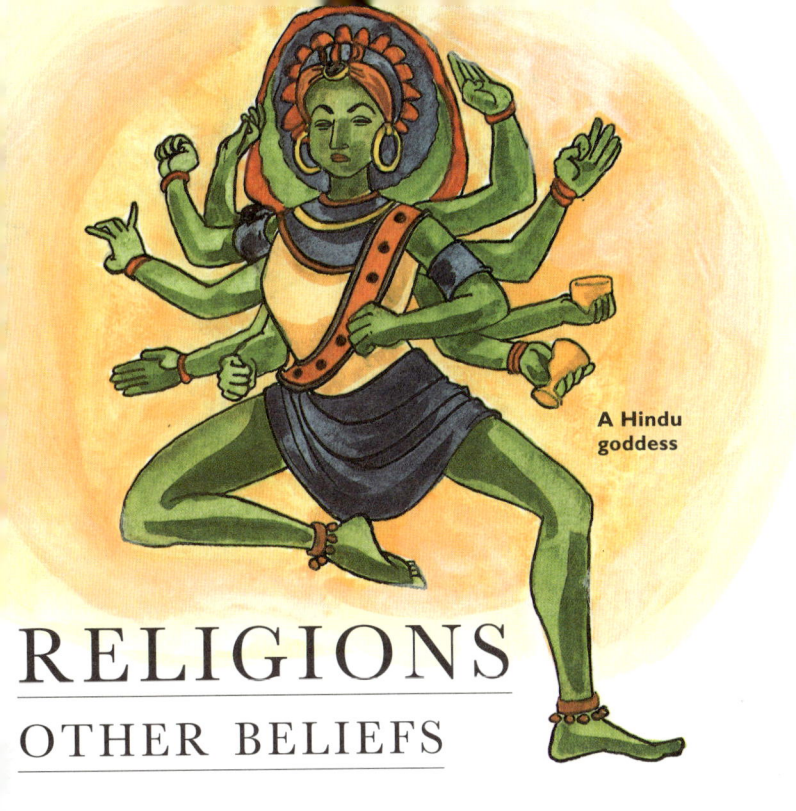

In the city of Athens, there were statues to many gods and goddesses. One day, Paul visited Athens. When he started to preach he said, 'I will tell you about the unknown God…this God wants people to search for him.' Then Paul went on to talk about Jesus.

SEARCHING

People today are looking for God through many different religions. In his sermon, Paul showed that other religions may have glimpses of the truth, but he believed that Jesus brought the full truth about God.

John said: 'Test the teachers to see if they come from God. Have nothing to do with those who do not teach the truth.'

A Greek goddess

BUDDHISM

Buddhists follow the teachings of Buddha. Their aim is to find perfect peace (nirvana) by following an eight-fold path of right living.

Buddha

HINDUISM

Hindus worship many different gods. They believe that after death, you are born again in another body. The type of body you are reborn in depends on how good you have been in this life.

Hindus believe that you can be reborn in another body

ISLAM

Muslims believe that Jesus was a good teacher sent by God, but the greatest teacher was Muhammed.

JUDAISM

Jews believe God made an agreement with their ancestor Abraham, that Jews should teach God's laws to the world. They believe that one day God's messenger will come to change the world.

SECTS

Many religious groups say that they follow some, or even all, of the teaching of the New Testament. Two well-known non-Christian sects are Mormons and Jehovah's Witnesses.

Bible Search

- Testing: *1 John 4:1–3; 2 John 9–10*
- Trust: *Galatians 2:16*
- Obedience: *Matthew 7:21*

SUFFERING

Looking to the Bible for answers

One of the hardest questions we ask is: 'Why is there so much suffering in the world?' The Bible only gives hints, not full answers. It does say that God is good, that he comforts those in need, and that one day he will bring all suffering to an end. Here are some of the Bible's comments.

THE DEVIL CAUSES TROUBLE

Job was a good man, who loved God. Then the Devil decided to test his faith, and Job lost everything. His seven sons and three daughters were killed, as were his 7,000 sheep, 3,000 camels and 1,000 cattle. He became seriously ill.

Job's wife told him, 'Curse God and die.' But Job would not say anything against God. Eventually, God made him even happier and richer than before.

Job lost everything

SELFISHNESS CAUSES FIGHTS

Much suffering in the world is because God has given us freedom to choose, and human beings make other human beings suffer. James said the reason for fights and quarrels was wanting something and not getting it.

Selfishness causes fights

WHOSE FAULT?

Some people think that illness is a punishment from God. This is not true. God can bring good out of it, but God does not cause it. A man who had been born blind was brought to Jesus. Jesus' friends said, 'Who sinned? Was it this man? Or was it his parents?' Jesus replied, 'His blindness has nothing to do with his sin or his parents' sin. He is blind so that God's power might be seen in him.'

Bible Search

- Paul: *2 Corinthians 1:3–4*
- Causes of fights: *James 4:1–6*
- A blind man: *John 9:1–41*
- The end of suffering: *Revelation 21:4*
- God doesn't cause evil: *James 1:13–17*

JESUS

God does not cut himself off from suffering. God sent his own son, Jesus, to die on the cross (a hideous way to die) so that he might destroy the power of sin, suffering and death.

Paul wrote: 'Praise be to the God and father of our Lord Jesus Christ…who comforts us in all our troubles, so that we can comfort those in any trouble…' We are to share God's comfort with people who suffer.

SUNDAY
A DAY OF REST?

Sunday is sometimes called 'the Lord's day'. It's the day when most Christians go to church.

There are issues about Sundays which concern some Christians. How should they spend the day? Can they work on a Sunday? Should shops stay open?

Should I work on a Sunday?

Should shops open on Sunday?

BEGINNINGS

In Genesis, we are told that God made the world in six days, and then rested on the seventh day. God then said that the seventh day should be a 'holy day'. This was written into the Ten Commandments. Jewish people call this day the Sabbath, and they celebrate it on Saturday.

JESUS

One Sabbath, Jesus' friends picked and ate some ears of corn. But this counted as work, and when some Pharisees noticed, they told Jesus it was wrong. In reply he said, 'The Sabbath was made for man, not man for the Sabbath.'

Jesus disagrees with the Pharisees

SUNDAY

Jesus was brought back to life on the first day of the week: Sunday. The first Christians started to meet together every Sunday to praise God for Jesus' resurrection. They held a communion service (the Lord's Supper), and collected money for people in need. But Sunday was still an ordinary working day, not a holiday.

The writer of the Letter to the Hebrews said that Jesus set people free from having to keep Jewish laws. Every day was now filled with the peace of the Sabbath.

THE CHRISTIAN CHURCH

Christians wanted to show that they didn't follow the Jewish faith. So they gradually stopped keeping the Jewish Sabbath. As time went on, church leaders told Christians to keep Sunday as a day for rest and worship. Sunday began to be called the Sabbath.

Paul advised, 'One man considers one day more important than another; another man considers every day alike… Do not judge your brother.' (See the pages on Church, Work, and Worship.)

Bible Search

- Paul's advice: *Romans 14:5; Colossians 2:16*
- Jesus: *Matthew 12:1–12*
- First Christians: *Acts 20:7; 1 Corinthians 16:2*
- Singing: *Ephesians 5:19*

69

SUPERSTITION
AND MAGIC

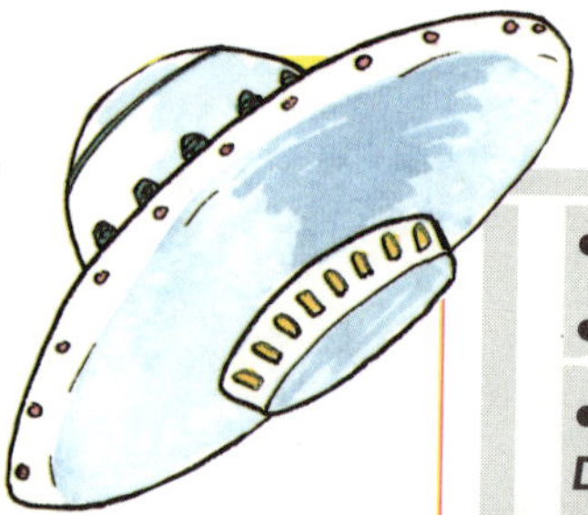

Some people enjoy studying the mysterious, and turn to things such as magic, reincarnation, aliens, UFOs, corn circles and 'new age' beliefs to bring meaning to their lives. Bible writers also had to deal with strange ideas, and they give us helpful guidelines.

Bible Search
- Jesus: **John 3:16; 14:6**
- A bonfire: **Acts 19:19**
- Forbidden magic: **Deuteronomy 18:9–13**
- God in control: **Psalm 37:3–5, 23–24**
- Useless astrologers: **Isaiah 47:13**

SUPERSTITION

A superstition is a belief, which is not based on anything true or real, that an object or an action will bring good or bad luck. Jesus set people free from superstition. He said, 'I am the way, the truth and the life.'

MAGIC

Magic, such as card and conjuring tricks, is harmless. But some people, who call themselves witches and sorcerers, practise black or white magic as a way of of getting power. They try to use magic spells to control other people or events. This sort of magic is forbidden in the Bible. To use magic is the opposite of trusting God.

Conjuring tricks are harmless

Some people are superstitious about walking under ladders

FORTUNE-TELLING

Fortune-telling is trying to find out what is going to happen in the future by looking at some sort of object, and taking a meaning from it. In the Bible, fortune-telling is called 'divination'. The Greeks studied the insides of dead birds to find out the future!

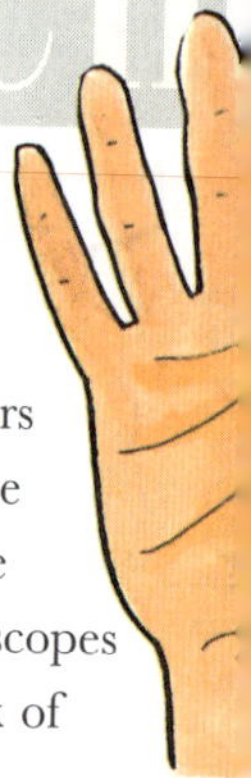

Fortune-tellers today may use cards, or study the palm of a person's hand. Astrologers aim to tell the future from the position of stars, and produce horoscopes. Relying on horoscopes to tell the future shows a lack of love and trust in God.

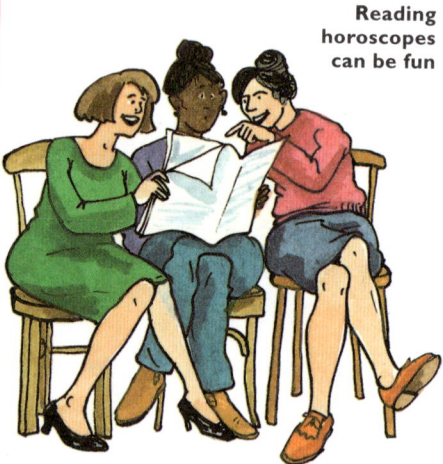

Reading horoscopes can be fun

STRANGE IDEAS

John wrote to advise Christians how to tell which mystical ideas were harmless, and which were dangerous. If the people teaching these ideas disagreed with any of the following statements, said John, their ideas were wrong.
- Jesus is God and died and rose again.
- Jesus brings love, forgiveness and peace to those who obey him.
- God is in control of all that happens.

70

TEMPTATION

Temptation is when an idea comes into our mind to do something we should not do. Jesus himself was tempted. The New Testament says: 'He was tempted in every way, just as we are, yet was without sin.' This verse shows that it's not wrong to be tempted, only to give in to the temptation.

THE CAUSE

James wrote, 'Never say "God is tempting me..." God does not tempt anyone.' Temptation comes from evil outside us, or from our own mixed-up natures. (Look at the page on the Devil.)

THE TEMPTATION OF JESUS

The Bible shows us two times when Jesus was tempted, and how he beat the temptation:

• With the Bible.
For forty days, Jesus prayed by himself in the lonely desert, and there the Devil tempted him. Each time a temptation came, Jesus hit back with a verse from the Bible. He used the Bible like a sword.

Jesus used the Bible like a sword

Jesus prays

• With prayer.
On the night Jesus was captured, he lay on the ground in the Garden of Gethsemene, and prayed to God. He asked God to spare him the death that was to come, if possible. But only if that was what God wanted.

CRASH

Everybody, except Jesus, gives in to temptation. What then? John told his friends what to do: if they confessed their sins, God would forgive them. We can trust God. He does what is right. He will make us clean from all the wrongs we have done.

If we confess our sins, God will forgive us

PETER

The night Jesus was arrested, the disciples became very scared. Peter was asked by three different people if he knew Jesus. But three times he swore that he did not. Later, Jesus forgave him and helped him to start again. Peter became one of the leaders of the Christian Church.

Three times, Peter denies knowing Jesus

Bible Search

• Jesus is tempted: *Matthew 4:1–11; 26:41*
• Jesus understands: *Hebrews 2:18; 4:15–16*
• Forgiveness: *1 John 1:9*
• The sword: *Ephesians 6:17*

TEN COMMANDMENTS

GOD'S LAWS

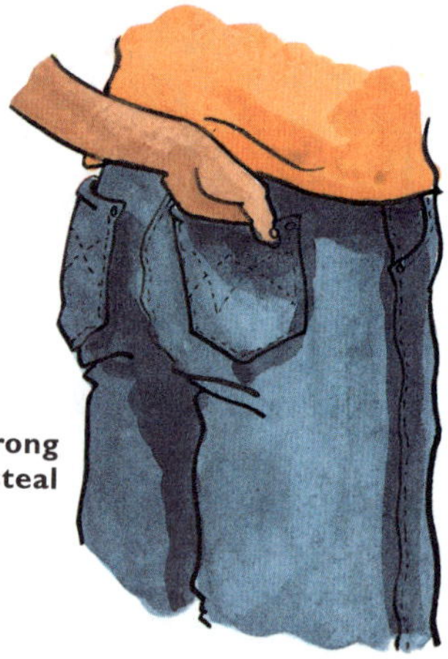

It is wrong to steal

God rescued the Israelites from slavery in Egypt. Now they needed guidance on how to live as God's people. Moses went up Mount Sinai, and there God gave him the Ten Commandments.

The commandments fall into two groups. The first four are about how to live with God. The second six are about getting on with other people.

THE TEN COMMANDMENTS

1. You shall have no other gods before me.
(God must come first in your life.)
2. You shall not make for yourself an idol in the form of anything in the heaven above, or the earth beneath, or in the waters below. You shall not bow down to them or worship them.
(You must not make any images to worship. God is invisible. You must worship only God.)

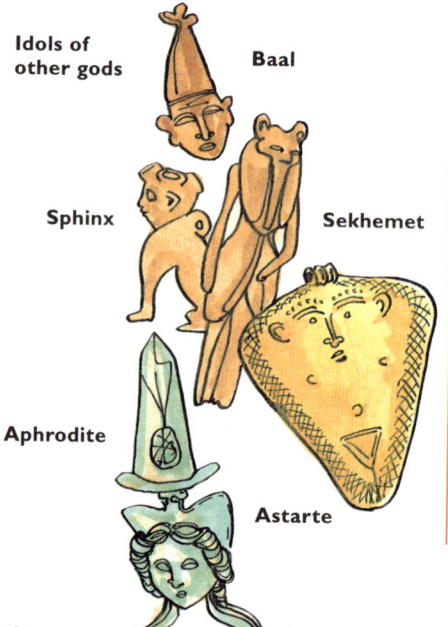

Idols of other gods
Baal
Sphinx
Sekhemet
Aphrodite
Astarte

3. You shall not misuse the name of the Lord your God.
(God's name is not a magic charm.) 
4. Remember the Sabbath day by keeping it holy.
(One day in seven is for rest and worship.)
5. Honour your father and mother.
(Respect your parents.)

Respect your parents

6. You shall not murder.
7. You shall not commit adultery.
(Do not have a love affair with someone else's husband or wife.)

8. You shall not steal.
9. You shall not give false testimony against your neighbour.
(You must not tell lies about anyone in a court of law.)
10. You shall not covet your neighbour's house....or anything that belongs to your neighbour.
(You must not long to have something that is not yours.)

A SUMMARY

One day, Jesus was asked which was the most important commandment. He quoted from two places in the Old Testament:
- 'Love the Lord your God with all your heart, and with all your soul, and with all your mind, and with all your heart.'
- 'Love your neighbour as yourself.'

In these words, Jesus summed up the Ten Commandments.

Bible Search
- Ten Commandments: *Exodus 20: 1–17; Mark 12: 28–31*
- Written on stone: *Exodus 24:12*

THANKS AND PRAISE

The words 'thanks' and 'praise' often come together in the Bible. We thank God because everything is a gift from him. Praising God means sharing in and showing the greatness and joy of God.

A psalmist wrote: 'Sing to the Lord with thanksgiving… He covers the sky with clouds; he supplies the earth with rain and makes grass grow on the hills. He provides food for the cattle… .'

Bible Search

- Psalms of praise: *Psalm 34, 135, 136, 145–150*
- In prison: *Acts 16:16–40*
- Thanks for everything: *Ephesians 5:20*

THANKS FOR EVERYTHING

Paul and Silas were beaten and thrown into prison. In prison they prayed and sang hymns to God. Paul wrote: 'Give thanks in all circumstances, this is God's will for you.' He also said, 'Make music in your hearts to the Lord, always giving thanks to God the Father for everything… .'

PAUL IN CORINTH

Jesus died on the cross and rose again. He did this to set us free from the power of evil. Paul said, 'Thanks be to God! He gives us the victory through our Lord Jesus Christ.' And Peter said, '…declare the praises of him who called you out of darkness into his marvellous light.'

PRAISE FOR COMFORT

Paul wrote: 'Praise be to the God and Father of our Lord Jesus Christ…who comforts us in all our troubles, so that we can comfort those in any trouble with the comfort we ourselves have received from God.'

PRAISE FOR HEALING

One day Jesus healed ten lepers. Nine went rushing off, but one came back to thank Jesus. 'Where are the other nine?' Jesus asked. 'Did they not want to praise God?'

SACRIFICE OF PRAISE

The Letter to the Hebrews says: 'Through Jesus, therefore, let us continually offer to God a sacrifice of praise… .' This means a sacrifice where we let go of what we want in order to do something for God.

THANKS FOR FRIENDS

Paul often wrote to his friends, 'We always thank God for all of you…', meaning that he thanked God for the good things about friends.

TRINITY OF GOD

Trinity is a way of describing God. The word was first used by early Christians. They said, 'God is one God. But he is not single. He is three: Father, Son and Holy Spirit.' God the Father, God the Son, and God the Holy Spirit are often called 'the persons of the Trinity'.

Bible Search
- Jesus' last orders: *Matthew 28:18*
- Jesus speaks to Philip about God's three dimensions: *John 14:9–12*
- Paul's trinitarian prayer: *2 Corinthians 13:14*

ONE GOD

God gave Moses the Ten Commandments, to show the Israelites how they must live. The first commandment said, 'I am the Lord your God…You shall have no other god.'

Other countries had lots of gods. One of the things that made the Jews special, was the fact that they worshipped one god.

In the Bible, the Holy Spirit is often represented as a dove

Jesus prays

THE FATHER

Jesus often went to a lonely place to pray. And when he prayed, he spoke to God as 'Father'. He taught his friends that God was their loving father.

JESUS

Jesus at the Last Supper

The night before he was arrested, Jesus and the disciples ate a last meal together. During the meal, Philip said, 'Show us the Father.' And Jesus replied, 'Anyone who has seen me, has seen the Father.'

After a little while, the disciples slowly became sure that Jesus was indeed God.

THE HOLY SPIRIT

Jesus' friends were praying in an upstairs room when the Holy Spirit came to them. They became sure that the Holy Spirit was truly God, carrying out his actions. (See the pages on the Holy Spirit.)

THE TRINITY

The Trinity is God the Father, God the Son, and God the Holy Spirit. The Trinity is not three separate gods, or one God with three different names. It means that God has three aspects, just as space has three dimensions of height, width and depth. The Hebrew word for God is 'Elohim', which is a plural word.

It is hard to understand the Trinity. But it is the only explanation that fits the facts in the Bible. Paul's prayer helps to make it clear. He said, 'The grace of the Lord Jesus Christ, the love of God, and the fellowship of the Holy Spirit be with you.'

TRUTH AND LIES

Truth is what is real. God is truth we can rely on. Many people can't face the truth about God. It was the same in Paul's day: 'They exchanged the truth of God for a lie,' said Paul.

Jesus said, 'I am the truth.' About the Devil, Jesus said, 'There is no truth in him. He is a liar and the father (the starting-point) of lies.'

JESUS

After his arrest, Jesus was eventually brought before Pilate, the Roman governor. Jesus said, 'Everyone on the side of truth listens to me.' 'And what is truth?' Pilate asked. He didn't need to hear a reply. He was staring at the truth: Jesus.

Jesus and Pilate

LIVING TRUTH

Jesus said, 'If you hold to my teaching you will know the truth, and the truth will set you free.' The way to experience truth is to obey Jesus. Paul called the good news about Jesus 'the word of truth'.

LIES

I didn't do it!

Bible Search

- What God wants: **Psalm 51:6**
- Lies instead of truth: **Romans 1:18–23**
- Word of truth: **Ephesians 1:13**
- Father of lies: **John 8:44**

It's my best one.

God doesn't love me.

RUBBISH!

Jesus was furious with those Pharisees who said they loved God, but whose actions were unloving. Their lives were a lie. 'You hypocrites!' said Jesus. The word 'hypocrite' means 'play-actor'. The Pharisees often said long prayers in front of people, hoping everyone was admiring them!

A HAPPY MAN

When Jesus first saw Bartholomew, he was sitting under a fig tree. Jesus described him as 'a true man in whom there is nothing false'. This was the highest praise.

A psalmist said, 'Happy the man in whose spirit there is no deceit (lies).' 'God wants inner truth,' said David.

WISDOM
'WISE AS SERPENTS'

Wisdom has nothing to do with being clever. It means that in our choices and actions, big and tiny, we should know and do what God wants.

Wise people were popular in Old Testament times, and advised people on many practical matters.

A serpent

Bible Search

- The start of wisdom: *Proverbs 9:10*
- Solomon's wisdom: *1 Kings 3:5–28, 4:29–34*
- A gift: *James 1:5*
- The cross: *1 Corinthians 1:20–24*

BE WISE

'Be innocent as doves, and wise as serpents,' said Jesus. How can we be wise? Jesus shows us. Paul wrote: 'In Jesus are hidden all the treasures of wisdom.'

THE WISE AND FOOLISH BRIDESMAIDS

Jesus told a story about ten bridesmaids. Ten young women were bridesmaids at a wedding. They were all due to carry lamps to light the wedding procession. Five bridesmaids were wise, and carried extra oil for their lamps. The other five were foolish and forgot to take any.

While the bridesmaids waited for the groom to arrive, the oil in the lamps ran out. The foolish bridesmaids had to go and buy more oil, and missed the wedding.

Jesus' story showed people that they should be well prepared for going to heaven.

SOLOMON THE WISE

When David died, his son Solomon became king of Israel. One night God spoke to Solomon in a dream. 'Ask me for whatever you want,' God said. What an offer! Solomon asked God for the wisdom to rule his country.

The Hebrew word for wisdom means 'a listening ear'. The first step towards wisdom is to hear what God is saying.

A CASE STUDY

Soon afterwards, two women came to Solomon for advice. They were having a violent row over a baby. Each woman said the baby was hers.

'Cut the baby in two,' said Solomon.

'That's fair,' said one woman.

'No. Give her the baby,' said the second woman.

Solomon then knew that the second woman must be the real mother, and gave the baby to her.

Two women fight over a baby

The wise and foolish bridesmaids

WOMEN

Women and girls form half the world's population. Yet they own less than one hundredth of the world's property. In many parts of the world, women do not get an education.

The teaching of the New Testament states that women and men are equal, and must be given equal rights.

Bible Search
- Adam and Eve: *Genesis 1:27–28*
- No difference: *Galatians 3:28*
- Priscilla: *Romans 16:3*
- Witnesses: *Mark 16:1–8*
- Mary: *Luke 10:42*

A female priest

ADAM AND EVE

In the first chapter of the Bible we read that God made both Adam and Eve in his image. They were both told to look after the world. Eve was called Adam's helper, but this did not mean that she was less important than him.

IN GOD'S SERVICE

In the Bible we learn of some female leaders, in charge of both men and women.
- Deborah was a judge of all Israel.
- Miriam was a prophetess, speaking God's word to the people.
- Many women helped the apostle Paul in his preaching work, including Priscilla. Paul described her as his co-worker.

Miriam

Paul and Priscilla

WOMEN IN THE CHURCH

Some Christians are against having female priests and ministers. They refer to a few Bible passages which speak of male 'headship', and point out that Jesus had twelve male apostles.

Other Christians say that some practical rules in the New Testament about women not teaching were to avoid unnecessary offence to customs of the time. For example, one of the apostles' jobs was to preach, and Jewish law would not allow women to preach.

JESUS

Women were among the close group of friends who travelled around with Jesus. By welcoming women into this group, Jesus was doing something revolutionary. In Bible times, women were considered less important than men. They were not allowed to be witnesses in a court of law. Yet the first people to witness Jesus' resurrection were women. This was a sign to all men! 'Go and tell the disciples,' said the angels.

Jesus and Mary

WORK

A workaholic

Work is an activity that earns money (or that trains you to earn money, like schoolwork!) Work is also any activity undertaken for a purpose. For example, in Christian life it is an activity that has spiritual results. True prayer is work.

A GIFT

Work was never meant to be a hard slog. It was a gift. The Garden of Eden was a place of perfect happiness, and God put Adam and Eve there 'to work it and take care of it'.

For Christians, what matters is not what you do, but the way you do it. Paul said, 'Whatever you do, work at it with all your heart as though you were working for the Lord and not for men.' And Paul wrote those words to slaves!

Work which is a call from God to serve him in the world, is called a vocation. Priests, vicars, nuns, ministers and preachers are all following a vocation. Sometimes this is paid work; sometimes it is voluntary.

A nun

UNEMPLOYMENT

Not having a job is depressing

Millions of people today can't get jobs. This is wrong, because work is an important part of human life.

Unemployment makes many people feel useless, but there are still things they can do. Our importance does not come from the job we do, but from our friendship with God. Every Christian can pray and serve God. This is work we can do for the whole of our lives.

ANY QUESTIONS
1 What is a vocation?
2 Why is it important for people to work, besides earning money?

REST

One day Jesus said to his friends: 'Come with me by yourselves to a quiet place, and get some rest.' Some people are workaholics, which means they can't stop working and rest. This is as bad as being lazy.

The writer of the Book of Proverbs made fun of lazy fools: 'A little sleep… a little folding of the hands to rest, and poverty will come on you like a bandit!'

Lazy fools

Bible Search
- A wicked lazy man: **Matthew 25:26**
- A gift: **Genesis 2:15**
- Hard work: **Genesis 3:17–18**
- Advice to slaves: **Colossians 3:22–23**
- Your aim: **1 Thessalonians 4:11**

Objects of worship?

WORSHIP TODAY

To worship someone or something means to be devoted to that person or object, giving them your greatest possible respect and love. Human beings have a built-in need to worship. Whatever people put first in their lives, is their object of worship.

Bible Search

- Keep meeting together: **Hebrews 10:25**
- Pray all the time: **1 Thessalonians 5:17**
- Worship with our lives: **Romans 12:1–2**
- Places don't matter: **John 4:21–26**

TRUE WORSHIP

Paul wrote: 'We are members of God's family, and I ask you to remember two things: keep God's kindness always in your minds; and give yourselves heart and soul to him, your energy, your heart and your mind. You belong to God, and it is service (worship) like this that makes God glad.'

Paul wrote that we should worship all the time. We are worshipping God when we try to please him in our lives, in our work, and in our choice of friends.

IN CHURCH

Christians belong to a family. They meet together with other members of the Christian family to worship God in church by:
- Singing.
- Prayer.
- Learning from Bible readings and sermons.
- Remembering the life, death and resurrection of Jesus.
- Sharing. Giving money to the collection is a sign that we want to help with God's work in the world.

Singing hymns

TRUTH

One day, Jesus sat down by a well and talked to a woman about worship. He said that the important thing was not where we worship, but our spirit of true love for God.

Jesus at the well

DIFFERENT FORMS

Worship in church can take many forms. Some services are very formal, some are very free. Many churches make the Holy Communion the centre of their worship.

Singing hymns or songs, listening to a choir, joining in prayers, watching a ceremony, are all part of worship. If one kind of worship does not appeal to you, another kind might.

79

INDEX

A

Abba, 29
Abortion, 16
Abraham, 5, 20, 66
Adam, 28, 53, 77, 78
Addiction, 18
Adultery, 53
Agnostics, 31
Agreements, 66
Ambition, 21
Angels, 5
Anger, 6
Animals, 7
Apostles, 8, 15
Archangels, 5

B

Balaam, 5, 7
Baptism, 8
Beatitudes, 37
Blasphemy, 56
Buddhism, 67
Bullying, 60

C

Caring, 26
Christianity, 9-11, 51, 69
Church, 12, 13, 38, 77, 79
Concentration, 63
Conversion, 9
Covenant, 66
Creation, 14
Creed, 15

D

David, 26, 53
Death, 16
Deborah, 77
Decision-making, 36
Demons, 27
Devil, 17, 68
Divination, 70
Divorce, 53
Doctrine, 13
Dreams, 35
Drugs, 18

E

Earth, 34, 58
Endurance, 44
Eucharist, 51
Eve, 28, 53, 77, 78
Evolution, 14
Exorcism, 27

F

Faith, 20, 37
Fame, 21
Families, 22
Fault-finding, 32, 68
Food, 18
Forgiveness, 23, 24
Fortune-telling, 70
Freedom, 25
Friends, 26, 73

G

Gambling, 18
Genesis, 14, 53, 69
Ghosts, 27
Gideon, 35
Giving, 28
God, 30, 31, 57, 77
  Grace, 33
  Kingdom of, 48
  Law, 72
  Names of, 30
  Trinity, 74
Gossip, 32
Governments, 50
Grace, 33
Greed, 28
Green issues, 34
Guidance, 35, 36

H

Happiness, 37
Healing, 38, 73
Health, 38
Heaven, 39
Hell, 39
Helping others, 58
Hinduism, 67
Holiness, 40
Holy Communion, 51
Holy Spirit, 12, 36, 41-3, 74
Hope, 44
Hospices, 16

I

Islam, 67
Israelites, 5, 30, 35, 38

J

James, 57
Jesus Christ, 6, 45-7, 53, 64, 69
  angels, 5
  baptism, 8
  Eve, 28, 53, 77, 78
  faith, 20
  families, 22
  forgiveness, 24
  freedom, 25
  friendship, 26
  God, 30
  grace, 33
  healing, 38
  helping others, 58
  Holy Spirit, 12, 13
  miracles, 54
  names, 56 
  peace, 58
  promises, 66
  resurrection, 77
  Romans, 50
  suffering, 68
  temptation, 71
  Trinity, 74
  truth, 75
  wisdom, 76
Job, 68
John the Apostle, 39, 50
Jonathan, 26
Joseph, 35
Judaism, 67
Judgement Day, 19
Judges, 29

K

Killing, 16
Kingdom of God, 48
Knowing yourself, 49

L

Law, 24, 72
Leaders, 50
Lies, 75
Lord's Prayer, 61
Lord's Supper, 51
Love, 33, 52

M

Magic, 70
Marriage, 53
Mary, 5
Mary Magdalene, 47, 64
Mass, 51
Miracles, 54
Miriam, 77
Money, 55
Moses, 66

N

Names, 29, 56
Nathan, 65
Nebuchadnezzar, 30
Need, 58
Noah, 66

O

Obedience, 57
Occult, 27

P

Passover, 51
Paul, 22, 73
Peace, 58
People in need, 58
Persecution, 60
Peter, 8, 50, 71
Pollution, 34, 44, 58
Praise, 73
Prayer, 61, 62, 63
Prejudice, 64
Priests, 65
Problems, 63
Promises, 66
Prophets, 65

Q

Questions, 62

R

Religions, 67
Rest, 78
Resurrection, 47, 77
Revelation, 39
Revenge, 60
Romans, 50
Rules, 25

S

Sacrifices, 73
Samaritans, 16
Science, 14
Scribes, 65
Second Coming, 19
Sects, 67
Self-knowledge, 49
Selfishness, 68
Shalom, 58
Sharing, 26
Signs, 35
Silas, 8
Sin, 23, 45
Solomon, 76
Suffering, 68
Sunday, 69
Superstition, 70
Swearing, 56

T

Taizé, 13
Taking, 28
Temptation, 71 
Ten Commandments, 72
Thanks, 73
Thomas, 31
Treasure, 48
Trinity, 74
Truth, 75, 79

U

Unemployment, 78

W

Wisdom, 76
Witnessing, 11
Women, 64, 77
Work, 78
World, end of, 19
Worship, 79

X

Yahweh, 29

Z

Zacchaeus, 28

80